AWAKENING
THE HERO
WITHIN
YOUNG ADULTS

Through Teaching and Preaching
the Narrative Story

Be A Hero!

2008

AWAKENING
THE HERO
WITHIN
YOUNG ADULTS

Through Teaching and Preaching
the Narrative Story

Rogers W. Jackson
B.A., M.Div., Th.M., D.Min.

Serve Your Generation

ROGERS W. JACKSON
Rogers Jackson Ministries Inc.

Website: www.rogersjackson.com
Email: rogersjackson@comcast.net
(773) 490 -7269

ISBN-13: 978-1-60414-036-1
ISBN-10: 1-60414-036-4

Cronos Press is an imprint of Fideli Publishing, Inc.
www.fidelipublishing.com

Introduction

This book finds its context in the Emmanuel Baptist Church of Chicago. This church was initiated under the ministry of Rev. Dr. Lacey Kirk Curry who led this congregation from January 1973 to January 2003. It was under the mentorship of Pastor Curry, in my young adult years, that he injected into my spirit the "Call of Heroic Action." This book is dedicated to Pastor Curry and all Preachers and Teachers who through Narrative Teaching and Preaching attempts to "Awaken the Heroic Ideal in Young Adults for Service and Social Transformation."

At present, the Emmanuel Baptist Church concern centers on the young adult population of the church continuing the ministry of service long established by them. Using an Inductive Method, I intend to present data about *"the heroic ideal"* from ***Neo-Jungian psychology*** and the *"idea of courage"* from ***Tillichian thought*** to assess the innate desire of young adults to participate in heroic actions "in" and/or "beyond" the congregation. The pragmatic problem is to demonstrate how preaching "narrative stories" on "the idea of the hero" can offer suggestive methods to give young adults ways to establish their own personal service and ministry "in" and/or "outside" the congregation.

Dedication

Much appreciation is given to those who
helped in this thesis on the Hero.

Rev. Dr. Lacey Kirk Curry
Dr. Mary McElroy
Rev. Albert Johnson
Rev. Donald Williams
Rev. Elton Green
Bro. Ricord Jackson
Bro. William Wyatt
Rev. Craig Walls
Rev. Joseph Henry
Dr. Jack Skiles
Dr. Marcus Cosby
Marquelle Redmond
Paul Stewart
The Young Adults of Emmanuel
The Senior Adults of Emmanuel

Contents

Introduction...v

Dedication vi

1. The Context 1

    The Homiletical Issue: Engaging Young Adults
        in the Heroic Idea of Transformational Service 2

    The Heroic Story in Comics... 2

    The Popeye Principle: Holy Discontent 5

    The Hero in Biblical Narratives 6

    The Particular Issue: How to Tell the Story? 10

2. The Psychological Theory: The Idea of the Hero...............13

    The Foundational Theory 14

    The Hero Consciousness 14

    Preach to Help Young People Take Action 19

    The Hero Defined 23

3. The Theological and Biblical Framework in which
      to Tell the Story 27

    Preach the Story to Encourage...................................... 27

    Biblical and Theological Foundations for Courage.......... 28

    The Significance of Courage in My Experience............... 31

    The Courage to Be a Servant....................................... 33

    The Courage to Be a Social Transformer 37

    The Hero as Social Transformer 39

4. The Project and its Rationale: The Method of
    Shaping the Story 43
    Narrative Preaching as a Method to Assist in
        Discovering Ones Identity and Vocation 44
    The Conclusions and Results of the
        Methodology: How to Tell the Story 48
5. The Significance for the Wider Audience...........................51
    The Preacher as Hero 51
    The Heroic Aspects of the Spoken Word......................... 52
    Two Young Adults and Their Heroic Actions 53
    Marquelle: Service 53
    Paul: Social Transformation 54
6. Conclusion: The Preacher and the Preaching Task 57
    The Preacher's Task: Heroism through Personal
        Relationship 57
    The Preaching Task 60
Bibliography...63
Appendix A: Church Location..69
Appendix B: Reflections from the Preaching Peer Group......71
Appendix C: Developing the Sermon Purpose......................75
Appendix D: Pre – Questionnaire: Interpreting the Bible
    Story...77
Appendix E: Post-questionnaire following sermon................79
Appendix F: Pre – Post questionnaire: Understanding
    God's Call..81
    Pre-questionnaire before sermon................................... 81
    Post-questionnaire following sermon............................. 82
Appendix G: Developmental Behavior in the
    Narrative Story 83
Appendix H: Frank Thomas' Method of Narrative
    Examination 85

Appendix I: Robert Alter's Method of Narrative
    Interpretation 87
Appendix J: H. Michael Brewer's Hero Hermeneutic 89
Appendix K: Who is a Hero?..91
Appendix L: THE CALL TO BE A HERO!........................95
    Sermon Purpose: 95
Appendix M: Sermon Outlines on Service and Social
    Transformation..107
Appendix N: You Can Be a Hero Too!................................121

One

The Context

This preaching project is located in a small African American congregation on the southwest side of Chicago in the Auburn Gresham community. Since the church's organization in 1973, the church has become a predominate congregation of senior adults ages 65 and above. At present, the leadership of the congregation is headed by senior and median adults. The question before the congregation is *"Where do young adults (18 – 35) fit in the church's mission of service and social transformation?"*

In my years as pastor of this congregation, young adults have asked me about helping them find their purpose and place in congregational ministry. The questions of these young adults about their purpose and place and the concern of the older adults, as to who would carry on the work of congregational ministry began to connect. During this preaching initiative, it has been suggested that the biblical narrative stories, of young people, just like the above, hold the key to their "identity and vocation," and their "service" and "social transformation."

The Homiletical Issue: Engaging Young Adults in the Heroic Idea of Transformational Service

The **particular issue** in this church's context lies in how to engage and involve young adults in the church's "inside" ministry of service and "outside" ministry of social transformation? How can young adults "be," and "feel" a part of the church's life, history, and ongoing story of service and social transformation? How can young adults find the meaning of their lives through heroic action? In what way can young adults hear, in new ways, the witness of the biblical narratives of young heroes who gave themselves in service for the benefit of others?

The **hypothesis** is that young people desire to be heroic. They desire to *"be a part of a story"* that is transformative, or they want to *"hear a story"* where someone's life counted for something and made a difference. The call to **the heroic ideal** is foundational to the reclaiming of young adults to an "inside" and "outside" work and service of church ministry.

The Heroic Story in Comics

We are people who live in the hope of possibility. In spite of the disasters and the tragedies of our experiences, the hope of "light at the end of the tunnel" pervades our consciousness. We declare that there is a "silver lining" in every thunder cloud. This idea of hope for *the possibility of life* resides not only in adults, but young adults. Their hopes of possibility are witnessed when they tell us what they would like to do with their lives and what they would like to become.

The gift of hope in young people is *to dream and look for the good* in life despite the trial and trouble that is ever present and prevalent in their experiences. Preaching narrative stories has as its intention to address the idea of hope through biblical characters who in "dead end" and "no way out" situations, persevered in helping themselves and others get "unstuck" and moving again. Their actions of triumph were heroic. It is asserted that **preaching the idea of the hero** from the biblical narratives can be used as **foundation** on which young people can gain **courage** to "get on with the business" of their lives.

In a fascinating book titled <u>Who Needs a Superhero?</u>, the following insights have proven helpful to assist the preacher in "telling the story" of biblical hero[ine]s to recapture the mind of a generation who are caught up in the heroic ideal found in the comic strips and movies.

H. Michael Brewer has noted that "Religion is the deepest expression of our longing for a savior. Every heroic saga, legend, and myth is ultimately a variation on one universal story: When all seemed lost, a hero stepped in to rescue us from the evil around and within us."[1] Brewer further elaborates that The spiritual hunger for heroes is woven into the fabric of the human creature. Our Maker built us with a persistent longing for a rescuer who will save

---

[1] H. Michael Brewer, *Who Needs a Superhero? Finding Virtue, Vice, and What's Holy in the Comics* (Grand Rapids, MI: Baker Books, 2004), 10.

us from injustice and suffering./ In our bleakest moments, we pray for someone to save us from ourselves.[2]

Leo Partible has observed that young adults are "trying to cope with underachievement and disappointment."[3] Young "people are looking for answers to the big questions, like "What am I doing here?/ . . . only comic books did a better job of giving me answers than many of the sermons I heard."[4] The comics offer action, a world of good and evil where a person could exercise their unique gifts with courage and save the day.[5]

Why are "hero stories" important? Partible asserts that our experience in the world leads us to believe that we are "insignificant, [but] we need to know we are here for something greater. We need to be pushed to strive for big ideals and bigger dreams."[6] It is the experience of both young and old that "We live in a scary world, and hero stories express our longing for safety and security."[7] With situations and disasters beyond our control, we long for – someone [to] walk beside us to see us through the perils of life/ . . . So we keep looking for heroes./ When real heroes [leaders, doctors, police, and firefighters] let us down, we turn to the fictional variety.[8]

---

[2] Brewer, 10.

[3] Leo Partible in H. Michael Brewer, *Who Needs a Superhero? Finding Virtue, Vice, and What's Holy in the Comics* (Grand Rapids, MI: Baker Books, 2004), 5.

[4] Ibid., 6.

[5] Ibid.

[6] Ibid., 7

[7] Ibid., 9.

[8] Ibid.

Brewer notes that the stories of comic books offer "heroism, idealism, and sacrificial nobility . . ."[9] and these comic heroes serve to spark our imagination, but they are fictional. Comics awaken in the reader the inner belief and hope that love, justice, and good triumph in the face of the realities of disorder and chaos.

The Popeye Principle: Holy Discontent

The preacher who preaches heroic biblical narratives must bring to the story what Frank Thomas calls "sense appeal."[10] "Sense Appeal" moves us from the intellectual analysis of the "story" to the "emotional process" and "experience" of the story that stimulates us to "feel" we are in the story.[11] Through "sense appeal," the story becomes "concretized, personalized, memorable, and . . . understandable."[12] The story is no longer boring. Our senses are stirred, our emotions are released, our interest is sustained, and we are challenged by the story to respond and bring about a change where possible.[13]

It is at this point of "experiencing" the story that the hearer gains a *"holy discontent"*[14] with their situations and the conditions of others who are "stuck" in their existential

---

[9] Partible, 10.

[10] Frank Thomas, *They Like to Never Quit Praisin' God* (Cleveland, OH: United Church Press, 1997), 36 – 39.

[11] Ibid., 36.

[12] Ibid., 37.

[13] Ibid.

[14] Bill Hybels, *Holy Discontent: Fueling the Fire that Ignites Personal Vision* (Grand Rapids, MI: Zondervan, 2007).

predicament. Preaching *"the story"* moves the listener to the *"Popeye Moment"*[15] or *"The Popeye Principle."* The "Popeye Moment" is the time of rescue. It is the time of positive action that sets people free.[16] The "Popeye Moment" states, "That's all I can stands, and I can't stands no more!"[17] The *"Popeye Principle"* affirms that after an individual sees the conditions that hold life captive, [s]he becomes frustrated with the way things are and is moved to get involved in doing something to make right what has gone wrong in their world and context.[18]

Through *"telling the story"* of *biblical heroic personalities* the listeners gain a *"holy discontentment"* which begins to connect them with the "priorities of God/ . . . the very thing God wants to use to fire them up to do something, that under normal circumstances, they would never attempt to do."[19] "Telling the story" of biblical heroic figures can awaken the listener to *hearing and living* God's call to be heroic thus allowing them to find significance and purpose in the context of their lives.

The Hero in Biblical Narratives

The *hero*, in biblical narratives, is highlighted by the Jewish scholar, Robert Alter. He asserts that within the Hebrew Scriptures (Old Testament), *the hero* is seen in "a

---

[15] Hybels, 23.
[16] Ibid., 20.
[17] Ibid., 22.
[18] Ibid., 23.
[19] Ibid., 25.

series of recurrent narrative episodes."[20] Within the biblical text is witnessed "the careers of biblical heroes."[21] These biblical models of the hero in scripture are there to tell a story that happened in that historical biblical context, and gives us a fundamental framework of our *heroic careers and purposes* in the world.

Alter emphasizes that "biblical narrative characteristically catches its protagonists [heroes] at the critical revealing points in their lives."[22] Like the heroes in scripture, this narrative method asserts that we, and young adults, are called to be "protagonists" [heroes] who go forth in our "career[s] in a foreign region"[23] and "a foreign land"[24] to meet and transform the *structural and spiritual powers* that hold people captive.

The hero, in the narrative story, regardless to how "sinister the dangers looming over him[her], leads a charmed life, that . . . will always in the end prove him[her]self to be more of a [*power*] than the [*spiritually demonic powers*][25] that seek to dominate and control us. To face the demonic powers, *the hero*, through "the Bible's narration and through dialogue"[26] gives young adult listeners *illustrations*

---

[20] Robert Alter, *The Art of Biblical Narrative* (Berkeley, CA: Basic Books, 1981), 51.

[21] Ibid.

[22] Ibid., 51.

[23] Ibid., 60.

[24] Ibid., 52, 51, .

[25] Ibid., 48.

[26] Ibid., 69.

of how their lives are "confronted with alternatives"[27] to assist them in facing the negative powers and transform them.

It is further observed that scripture offer and present ***hero narrative "type – scenes"*** [28]that show the emergence of the hero. These "type scenes" can help young adults realize that ***in the ordinary situations of life*** God can awaken them to action, just as those in the biblical narrative were awakened to transform their world. The ***hero narrative "type - scenes"*** reveal the following:

1. They show "fixed conventions of the birth of the hero"[29] (Sarah births Issac, Hannah births Samuel, Elizabeth births John the Baptist).

2. The future hero is encountered at a well[30] (***Moses*** meets Reuel's daughters at a well and drives off the hostile shepherd (Ex. 2:15b – 21), Issac re-digs the wells of Abraham (Gen. 26:18ff), ***Jesus*** meets a woman at a well and gets her going again (John 4:5ff).

3. The hero sees God in the desert[31] (***Moses*** at the burning bush (Ex. 3:1 – 4), ***Jacob*** in the desert (Gen. 28:10 – 18).

4. The hero emerges out of the immediate family

---

27 Alter, 69.
28 Ibid., 51.
29 Ibid.
30 Ibid.
31 Ibid.

circle[32] (***Gideon*** is called to lead Israel (Judges 6:11 – 16), ***David***'s anointing as Israel's future king as the youngest in his family (1 Sam. 16:12), ***Ruth***'s heroism (Ruth 1:16ff).

5. The hero goes through an initiatory trial[33] (***Joseph***, the future leader of Egypt (Gen. 37:23ff, 39:1ff), the Lord ***Jesus*** tempted by Satan (Matthew 4:1ff).

The story narrative can help young adults examine the particular aspects of their lives as well as to learn how to analyze their story by assessing their setting, their actions, their feelings, their plot, their conclusions,[34] their resolutions, and their future vocations and careers in service and social transformation.

Everyone loves to hear a good story. Stories stimulate the imagination. Stories cause us to identify with the major and minor characters in the narration. Stories bring us into the situation and complications of the story as it unfolds. Stories raise in us an anticipation that whatever the conflicts, the tragedies, and the uncertainty in the narration a resolution is possible. In the story, we look for the "heroic" person who saves the day, who brings life to the barrenness, who brings transformation to the decimation, who brings a reversal to the tragedy, and who brings hope to the despair.

---

[32] Alter, 52.

[33] Ibid., 51.

[34] Eugene Lowry, *The Sermon* (Nashville, TN: Abingdon Press, 1977), 23.

"Preaching the story" of the hero can empower young adults to realize that they can "be a hero too" as they assume "heroic service" "in" and "beyond" the church walls. When I was an adolescent and a young adult in the church, I would hear people shout out when the preacher preached, "Tell the Story!" The story that was anticipated was how "Jesus would make a way out of a no way situation." As I grew older, I wanted to hear the story, and I would shout to the preacher, "Tell the Story!"

By "telling the story" of the biblical narrative, young adults can be awakened to the realization that God is calling them to take hold of actions that can help people get through what they are going through. Whatever the action, whether service "in the church institution" or "outside" of the church, in a secular setting, their heroic response to God's call will benefit and be a rescue to others.

The Particular Issue: How to Tell the Story?

In view of the above concern, the questions to be addressed are, "How can the preacher tell the story" to encourage Young Adults to have an "optimistic vision about [their] possibilities for [service]?"[35] How can they be serviceable to their culture?[36] In what way can they **break out of "prescribed social roles"**[37] given by the institutional

---

[35] Carol Pearson, *The Hero Within* (New York, NY: Harper Collins Publishers, 1989), xv.

[36] Ibid., 1.

[37] Ibid., 1.

congregation? How can they use their gifts and a
be of service in their world?

The preacher should ***intentionally interact and
dialogue*** with young adults about narrative stories both
biblical and social that address their "unconscious" desire
to produce, contribute, assist, and make a difference in
their context. How can "telling the story" ***awaken the
hero within*** young adults so that they can "listen to" and
"answer" ***God's call to a vocation of heroic service and
social transformation?***

It is not up to the preacher to tell young adults
what type of service they are to do in their context
of ministry. Yet, it is the preacher's task to tell them
that ***they are called to be serviceable.*** They are to be
serviceable because ***each is gifted*** to contribute to the
world to which they belong. Each has a contribution,
as those before them, who have enriched and enlivened
their world. The preacher, through the biblical story,
allows God's Spirit to direct young people in the area of
their interest, skill, and ability. Their actions of service
must be Spirit driven and directed, not preacher driven.
The preacher, whose intentions are good, is limited. The
faith of the preacher must be in the eternal mind and
purpose of God to bring to fullness the creative desire
God has for the young listener.

The biblical narratives alert us to the realization that
the Spirit of God who calls young people will give them
the empowerment and the methods whereby they will do
service. As young adults hear the biblical stories, it is hoped

that they will begin their journey of ***becoming participants*** in "heroic initiatives" that lead them to meaning and purpose for their lives.

Two

The Psychological Theory:
The Idea of the Hero

The central theory of Carol Pearson in <u>The Hero Within</u> and the <u>Awakening the Heroes Within</u> informs and motivates the idea that young adults can serve and bring social transformation to their world. From our childhood, adolescence, and even adulthood, we are fascinated with heroes in Westerns, Action Movies, Dramas, and even Cartoons. In the 2004 movie "Spider Man 2," Peter Parker (Spider Man) had given up his role of service as a hero. He wanted to be normal and common. In a conversation with his aunt (who did not know that he was Spider Man), she stated that people were wondering where Spider Man had gone. She told Peter that people needed heroes. She said, "There is a hero in all of us." In an article titled "The Ethics of Superheroes," the following heroic ideal is reaffirmed,

> What is the heart of the ethics of superheroes?
> It is the notion of a Calling (sometimes it goes
> by other names, e.g., freely-chosen Destiny).
> One of the more insightful posts I have seen
> on the ethics of *Spider Man 2* is . . . To be a

superhero is to be called to live a life apart in the service of higher things (in particular, the saving of others).[38]

The Foundational Theory

The ***foundational theory*** for preaching narrative stories is not to transform the listener into a super hero, but to reveal that at ***the core of our psychological self*** is the realization that "there is a heroic consciousness in all of us." In the book, The Hero with a Thousand Faces, Joseph Campbell asserts that throughout the history of civilizations myths and fairy tales have revealed the awakening of a hero who was assisted "through the trials and terrors of the weird adventure" by a wise old person.[39] "The hero," asserts Campbell, "is the man or woman who has been able to battle past his[her] personal and local . . . limitations/ . . . [to] visions, ideas, and inspirations [that] . . . spring of human life and thought."[40]

The Hero Consciousness

Campbell purports that ***the hero consciousness*** is "eternal" or a part of the "psychological self" when he notes, "The hero has died as a modern man; but as eternal [wo]man . . . universal [wo]man [s]he has been reborn./ .

---

[38] Siris: The Ethics of Superheroes, (Thursday, July 08, 2004) accessed 21 July 2007, <http://branemrys.blogspot.com/2004/07/ethics-of-superheroes.html>.

[39] Joseph Campbell, *The Hero with a Thousand Faces* (Princeton, NY: Princeton University Press, 1949), 9.

[40] Ibid., 20.

. . to return to us, transfigured, [to] teach the lesson [s]he has learned of life renewed."[41]   It is here that Campbell asserts ***the hero consciousness*** is embedded in the "psyche of culture" that is expressed in literature of various cultures through myth and stories.

The ***hero***, in ***Greek mythology*** and other stories, "give us courage to face the Minotaur [a bull headed man], and the means then to find our way to freedom when the monster has been met and slain."[42]   In world literature and narratives, ***the hero is an ordinary person*** who does extraordinary things as [s]he comes along side of those in difficulty and gets them unstuck from their situation and gets them going again.

Why is the hero a part of the human psyche? The hero is part of our psychological make up because each of us long for the "happy ending."   Because of the tragedies of life that shatter all forms of our reality, the "mythological hero" reaches into ***the inner depths of our psyche*** "where obscure resistances are overcome, and long lost, forgotten powers are revivified, to be made available for the transfiguration of the world."[43]   If there were no heroes to help us revive and transform our world, our psychological makeup would cause us to create a hero. Robert Moore, Professor of Spirituality and Theology at the Chicago Theological Seminary, Chicago, Illinois observes that the ***soldier – hero*** is an ***"archetype"*** lodged in the deep structures of our

---

[41] Campbell, *Hero*, 20.

[42] Ibid., 23.

[43] Ibid., 29.

psyche who is in a never ending quest to oppose forces that contend and quest for dominance.[44] Where ever there is a combat, the ***soldier – hero*** is in the life drama "at all times in history . . . here and now."[45]

Within all of us is the desire to be a "champion" who seeks to bring "harmony" to the dialectics, conflicts, chaos, and destruction[46] in our context. Moore suggests that ***in the "stories" of cultures*** the "soldier – hero" brings order to the chaos of life. The hero, in a story "allow[s] people to participate intentionally in the eternal, archetypal presence of the cosmic combat."[47]

Based on the above assertions, ordinary people each day participate in the heroic ideal. We are heroes when we are inspired "to live an empowered life in the service of [our] fellow creatures/ . . . mobilized for action, ready to charge forward to meet life head – on."[48] In the sermon, "Take Your Place with the Bruised,"[49] the young people and young adults shared with me their ordinary acts to live an empowered life in the service of others. These acts I classify as heroic:

---

[44] Moore and Gillette, *The Warrior Within* (New York, NY: William Morrow and Company, Inc., 1992), 89.

[45] Ibid., 91.

[46] Ibid., 93.

[47] Ibid.

[48] Ibid., 100.

[49] This sermon was preached Sunday, August 26, 2007 for the class on "Preaching for Social Transformation," taught at Lutheran School of Theology, Chicago, Illinois as a part of the Doctor of Ministry in Preaching Program.

o "I have a desire to help the homeless."

o "I participate in service through the Girl Scouts."

o "I deliver food to senior citizens."

o "I help clean city parks."

o "I share in a Saturday reading enrichment program for inner city youth."

o "I am a volunteer in getting blood drive donations."

o "I mentor children through praise dance."

o "I help in Boy Scouting."

o "I am trying to bring other young people to church."

o "I mentor girls at a local elementary school in self-esteem, anger management, and communication."[50]

Others responded that they will transform their world in the following ways –

o "I will use my gifts and talents to encourage the broken."

o "I will visit and pray for the sick on a regular basis."

o "I will tell others about God."

o "I am going to college to be a pediatrician to find a cure for sickle cell anemia."

o "I will tell others on my college campus that they

---

[50] This was a ***pre-questionnaire*** before the sermon "Take Your Place" that asked young people and young adults – ***"What type of service are you doing to help the community and society?"*** August 12, 2007.

> have a purpose and a place in the world and the
> Bible can help them find it."

o "I will be more observant of peoples' feelings and
help them through their situations."[51]

Given the "heroic consciousness" within each of us,
beginning in adolescence and young adulthood, young
adults have a desire to be "called forth" and "awakened" to
heroic responsibility beginning in the context of the local
congregation and then moving beyond it.

In my adolescence, I had a desire to serve the church. I
asked, "How could I serve and be of service to the church?"
As I matured into young adulthood, I had a desire to make
a contribution to the wellbeing of the society. Even then I
did not have clarity of purpose nor a clear call to do it. My
vision and vocation came as I listened to the preaching and
ision of the Rev. L. K. Curry,[52] an older pastor in Chicago,
IL. Through his telling me "the story," I was "awakened"

---

[51] These were responses from the young people of our
congregation to a ***pre – questionnaire*** in preparation for the
sermon "Take Your Place with the Bruised," Luke 4:16 – 18. The
question was ***"How will you serve and in what way do you hope to
transform your world?"***

[52] I met Pastor L. K. Curry in November of 1982. He gave me
a vision and a challenge to work with him in Christian Education
through the Emmanuel Christian School 8301 S. Damen Avenue,
Chicago, IL. At that time I did not know that an African American
Church could operate an elementary school. His challenge and his
story of how the Lord enabled him to start the Emmanuel Baptist
Church and School awakened in me the heroic ideal to which I began
the journey with him and I am still on the road seeking to meet the
challenges that are ahead.

to the work, service, and social transformation that my life longed to be engaged. It is my hunch that other young adults have the same heroic desires and what they need is a "word from the Lord" through the preacher to help them answer their call.

Preach to Help Young People Take Action

One of the aims of preaching narrative stories to young adults is to "do something" in the listener, and to stir the hearer to "do something."[53] Allen suggests, that young adults must feel welcomed into the church's ministry of service. The preacher must push the congregation beyond her tendency of "contemplation" and "sacred tradition"[54] to invite young adults to engage in its ministry of service and social transformation.

Young people, in our church context have complained that *the church isn't doing anything* to which they can participate and is boring. Dr. Jack Skiles observes that young people are saying, "The church is not doing ministry as they would do it. We have unwittingly attempted to make young people fit into our program, our way, and have not given them the freedom to fit in their own way."[55] Young people have observed their real concern and their critique is

---

[53] Scriptures of call and service: Exodus 3:4, Exodus 8:1, 1 Samuel 3:10, Jeremiah 1:5, Luke 4:18 – 19, Ezekiel 37:1, Matthew 28:19 – 20, Mark 16:15, Acts 1:8.

[54] Ronald Allen, *Preaching and Practical Ministry* (St. Louis, MO: Chalice Press, 2001), 125.

[55] Jack Skiles, August 28, 2007, Advisor to this project made the above comments.

that ***the church's "spirituality" is not "action-oriented."***[56] Their question is "how can we become participators based on our giftedness and abilities?"

Many young adults end up leaving the local institutional church because it does not engage them in a great enterprise. The church's spirituality is defined as "maintain[ing] social structures that sustain life"[57] We must ask, how can we free young adults to be creative in their service to the church both "inside" and "outside" its walls? The question and quest of the preacher is how, through preaching the narrative story of heroic action, can young people be encouraged to take their place in the work of God that brings benefit and blessing to life.

The quest to get young adults "into the sanctuary" and then into the "secular society" will happen as we come to understand their psycho-social-spiritual needs. Once we realize their ***developmental psychological need*** and "desire . . . to ***make something work***, and to make it work well,"[58] then we can free them to find an ***"occupation"*** that is ***"significant"*** to them and encourage them to move in that direction in their own unique excellence."[59]

In most instances, their spiritual empowerment moves them to want to join in the struggle for liberation, to be involved in social witness, to work with the homeless, to

---

[56] Allen, 125.

[57] Ibid.

[58] Erik Erikson, *Identity: Youth and Crisis* (New York, NY: W. W. Norton and Company, 1968), 129.

[59] Ibid., 129.

build housing, and to visit the sick. The problem has been in the fact that the local congregation has not adequately nurtured young people in the spirituality of "action in life."[60] Doug Fields, in his book, <u>Purpose Driven Youth Ministry</u> states that we must begin the process of preparing young people on purpose for ministry and service. One of the challenges of the pastor and the congregation is to begin the process of helping young people find their place of service and social transformation and to establish preaching and teaching that reflects God's purpose.

Fields suggests that we begin by establishing in our youth and young people's ministry purposes that "develop" and "equip" youth for service versus coordinating events and programs. Our purpose must be to make disciples.[61] What must we do? We must begin giving our young people more than a baby sitting service and an occasional Bible study. We must do the following to help young people take their place:

1. Depend on God to show us the plan.[62]

2. Pray for persons who will allow God to work through them with youth.[63]

3. Be a model of passionate faith that will excite young people.[64]

---

[60] Allen, *Preaching*, 125 – 126.

[61] Doug Fields, *Purpose Driven Youth Ministry* (Grand Rapids, MI: Zondervan Publishing House, 1998), 18.

[62] Ibid., 33.

[63] Ibid., 35.

[64] Ibid., 28.

4. Ask why you are doing what you are doing? Are you preparing young people to develop their service on the purposes of God?

Fields states that a ministry with young people that is built on "tradition, personality, finances, people, or programs"[65] will not last. The driving force must be on God's intention. It is obvious that the pastor cannot do this work alone. Begin by preparing young people and adults to focus on biblical purposes for service and social transformation in 1). **Worship**: celebrate God's presence.[66] 2). **Evangelism**: share your faith.[67] 3). **Fellowship**: become a welcoming community.[68] 4). **Discipleship**: strengthen young people to mature and grow.[69] 5). **Ministry**: meet the needs of others in love.[70]

When young people observe how the above purposes are acted out in the life of biblical heroic characters, they can be motivated to fulfill the innate ***drive to be productive and competent*** in the world[71] with the aim of completing at they have produced.[72] Chris Hedges has asserted that young people are looking for definitions of who they are.

---

[65] Fields, 45.

[66] Ibid., 48.

[67] Ibid., 47.

[68] Ibid., 48.

[69] Ibid., 49.

[70] Ibid., 50.

[71] Erik Erikson, *The Life Cycle Completed* (New York, NY: W. W. Norton and Company, 1982), 75.

[72] Erik Erickson, *Childhood and Society* (New York, NY: W. W. Norton and Company, 1963), 258 - 259.

They want to be tested and proved. They want to discover their worth as human beings. They want to join a great enterprise. This desire beckons them forward[73] to service, social transformation, and heroism.

The Hero Defined

There are numerous definitions of what it means to be a hero. Moore and Gillette assert that a hero is a person who has the courage to "come up against any number of obstacles."[74] A hero takes "an impossible situation and turn[s] it into a fighting chance."[75] A hero "gives us a fighting chance, to live and flourish."[76] When we look at a hero, we are given "a sense of Mission" or "Calling," an awareness of being asked to transcend narrow Ego concerns by focusing on some special task."[77] In the book, <u>Who Needs a Superhero?</u> Brewer states,

> Ordinary people abound with heroism. . .
> quiet, overlooked people . . ./True heroism
> rarely involves front-page rescues. . . . A
> hero is anyone who uses his or her gifts to
> do what needs to be done in the service of
> God's world."[78]

---

[73] Chris Hedges, *War Is a Force That Gives Us Meaning* (New York, NY: Anchor Books, 2002), 84.

[74] Moore and Gillette, *The Warrior Within*, 107.

[75] Ibid.

[76] Ibid.

[77] Ibid., 110.

78 Brewer, *Superhero*, 118.

The **heroic awakening** that comes through "telling the heroic story," summons young people to be **"significant"** persons who assist others in **getting "unstuck" and started again**. The **task of the hero[ine]** is that of alleviating people from their difficulty so that they might get on with their lives.[79] Campbell defines the **hero** as one who brings light, understanding, and enlightenment to the mind and soul.[80] The hero is one who will not turn back regardless of the difficulty of the task. The hero brings a **social transformation** and **spiritual significance** to life. The hero brings maturity to the human condition.[81]

The **heroic consciousness** is further explicated by Kenda Dean who observes that young people "want to find something to live for that is worth dying for. They want to know if Christianity is worth dying for. Is it worth putting their lives on the line for?"[82] Preaching "the story of the heroic" can be the catalyst whereby young adults can begin their faith quest to be **serviceable**[83] in the world.

The key theorist who gives shape to **the idea of the hero consciousness** is Carol Pearson. She **redefines** the hero as any person who enables people to get **"unstuck."** Pearson affirms that we all carry within our psyche **"the heroic ideal"** to get out of our existential predicament; we have

---

[79] Pearson, *The Hero Within*, 1.

[80] Campbell, *The Hero*, 388.

[81] Ibid.

[82] Kenda Dean, *Practicing Passion: Youth and the Quest for a Passionate Church* (Grand Rapids, MI: William B. Eerdmans Publishing Company, 2004), 31.

[83] Ibid., 148 – 149; see Pearson, *The Hero Within*, 71.

the desire to help others get unstuck and to get on their way. Our ***heroic nature*** propels us to go on our journeys and claim our heroism. Our heroic conscious moves us to desire to make an essential contribution to the world.[84]

The ***hero ideal*** gives us a consciousness of optimism and possibility.[85] We have an innate desire to confront the "dragons," and the powers of non-life, in order to bring life and change to our world and context. To not take the risk and the journey beyond our prescribed roles is to feel empty and discouraged.[86] Preaching "the story of the heroic" purposes to ***awaken young adults*** to use their youthful powers to "take the risks" of bringing order and social transformation to their social context.

---

[84] Pearson, *Hero*, 2, xv.
[85] Ibid., xix.
[86] Ibid., 1.

Three

The Theological and Biblical Framework in which to Tell the Story

Preach the Story to Encourage

Efrem Smith, in <u>Raising Up Young Heroes</u> purports,

> God is in the business of using ordinary young people to do extraordinary things./ God is in the business of taking kids who are scared, shy and intimidated and giving them the ability to go public with their gifts and speak boldly.[87]

The "story sermon" can *"encourage"* young adults to take actions that move them toward bringing wholeness to their context. To have *courage* means to "to have

---

[87] Efrem Smith, *Raising Up Young Heroes: Developing a Revolutionary Youth Ministry* (Downers Grove, IL: InterVarsity Press, 2004), 14, 15.

confidence,"[88] "to be bold," and "to go out bravely."[89] How can preaching "the story" empower young adults to go out with courage and serve their world? Ronald Allen suggests that preaching can help young people have courage to take "action in life."[90] Preaching the story of biblical heroes should help young hearers to connect with God in the divine activity in their particular world.[91] The story can assist young adults in discovering their giftedness and power to take action, where they can offer service in a positive manner.[92]

Biblical and Theological Foundations for Courage

Within the biblical story are examples of persons who were fearful. Yet, in the story and the experience of fear, "someone" stood by them and encouraged and helped them to be courageous.

o **Deuteronomy 31:7**, Moses tells Joshua to be courageous as he assumes the leadership of Israel into the God's promised land.

o **Joshua 1:6ff** purports God's directive to Joshua to be courageous.

---

[88] Spiros Zodhiates, *The Complete Word Study Dictionary: New Testament* (Chattanooga, TN: AMG Publishers, 1992), 718.

[89] Geoffrey Bromiley, *Theological Dictionary of the New Testament* (Grand Rapids, MI: William B. Eerdmans Publishing Company, 1985), 315 – 316.

[90] Ronald Allen, *Preaching and Practical Ministry* (St. Louis, MO: Chalice Press, 2001), 124.

[91] Ibid., 124.

[92] Ibid.

o **Judges 4:6ff** Barak is hesitant to fight against the army of Sisera unless Deborah the judge and prophetess goes with him. She goes to give him courage.

o **1 Samuel 30:6** is a disaster in David's leadership to which he was about to be stoned. The scripture asserts that he "encouraged himself in the Lord."

o **1 Chronicles 28:20** is David's farewell address to Solomon to be courageous as he becomes king of Israel.

Paul Tillich, in Volume One of his systematic theology, Reason and Revelation: Being and God, asserts that "courage" is the way we face the threat of nonbeing.[93] Courage is the power not to "surrender to the annihilating [powers in life]."[94] It is the power to provide and preserve my space, my physical location, my sphere of influence, my home, and my world.[95] Courage, according to Tillich, is the power "of self-affirmation even in the extreme state of radical doubt,"[96] insecurity and uncertainty. In Tillich's The Courage to Be, he affirms that the "ground of courage" and confidence is seen in "self-affirmation."[97] This idea of "self-affirmation," in courage, is significant for the heroic

[93] Paul Tillich, *Systematic Theology: Three Volumes in One*, Vol. 1 (Chicago, IL: The University of Chicago Press, 1967), 189.

[94] Ibid., 194.

[95] Tillich, *Systematic Theology: Three Volumes in One*, Vol. 1, 194.

[96] Tillich, *Systematic Theology: Three Volumes in One*, Vol. 2, 12.

[97] Paul Tillich, *The Courage to Be* (New Haven, CT: Yale University Press, 1952), 20.

conscious because the person needs to "self affirm," with confidence, that "God is with them" even in the face of their own "anxiety" about the possibility of their death[98] as they face of demonic powers.

In *Luke 22:42*, the Lord Jesus who was facing the cross of Calvary where He would engage the demonic powers of negation and nonbeing, prayed "Father, if thou be willing, remove this cup from me: nevertheless not my will, but thine, be done." In the moment of His anxiety about death, the Lord Jesus Christ affirmed courageously that God was present to enable Him to fulfill His heroic task. Dr. Martin Luther King, Jr., in <u>Strength to Love</u>, asserts,

> God does not forget his children who are victims of evil forces. He gives them the interior resources [courage] to bear the burdens and tribulations of life./ He imbues us with the strength needed to endure the ordeals, . . . and he gives us the courage and power to undertake the journey ahead./ . . he restoreth our souls, giving us renewed vigor to carry on.[99]

Courage is the power to "strive" and "persist" [100] and to never "surrender to the annihilating character of"[101] life. The hero needs courage that is the affirmation of life, the

---

[98] Tillich, *Systematic, Three Volumes in One*, Vol. 2, 193.

[99] Martin L. King, Jr., *Strength to Love* (Philadelphia, PA: Fortress Press, 1963), 85.

[100] Tillich, *Courage*, 20.

[101] Tillich, *Systematic, Three Volumes in One,* Vol. 2, 194.

affirmation of "self – preservation" and "other" preservation. Courage pushes us to "overcome" that which threatens or denies our lives and the lives of others.[102]

The Significance of Courage in My Experience

This idea of courage was significant to me because in my adolescence and young adulthood, I had many experiences of "existential fear" that still loom in my consciousness. My encounter with "fear" has led me to believe that **the word from the preacher**, though **narrative** and **contextual stories**, can help young people gain the courage to affirm who they are in the face of fearful situations, to enable them to strive forward in times of anxiety, insecurity, uncertainty, and even the meaningless moments of their lives with the certitude that "God is with them" to help them endure and to make their journey with courage.

The **significant piece** that has led me to **preach the idea of courage** through biblical narrative has its beginnings in the testimony of Dr. Martin King, Jr. in the sermon, "Our God is Able." Here, Dr. King is a young adult man who with his "heroic consciousness" experiences the "anxiety" of fear and death as he leads the Montgomery, Alabama bus boycott in 1955. It is through his narrative story, that I, as

---

[102] Tillich, *Courage*, 26 – 27.

a young adult, gained courage to accept my call to service and social transformation.[103]

> After a particularly strenuous day, I settled in bed . . . when the telephone rang. An angry voice said, "Listen, . . . Before next week you'll be sorry you ever came to Montgomery."/ It seemed that all of my fears had come down on me at once./ I was ready to give up. I tried to think of a way to move out of the picture without appearing to be a coward./ I determined to take my problem to God.

> "I am here taking a stand for what I believe is right. But now I am afraid. The people are looking to me for leadership, and if I stand before them without strength and courage, they too will falter. I am at the end of my powers./ At that moment I experienced the presence of the Divine . . . inner voice, saying, "Stand up for righteousness, stand up for truth. God will be at your side forever."

---

[103] It was the spring of 1975. I was a student at Bishop College, Dallas, TX. A young minister on the campus named Johnny Bowen asked me what God was doing with my life. As a 17 year old, I could not answer. He told me to pray and ask God to reveal to me my purpose and assignment. Through prayer, I received a call to preach, but declined through fear and uncertainty. I heard the voice of God tell me not to be afraid, "If you go, I will be with you." I am preaching today from that experience of the divine infusion of courage into my spirit on a Sunday morning in March of 1975.

> Almost at once my fears began to pass from me. My uncertainty disappeared. I was ready to face anything. The outer situation remained the same, but God had given me inner calm.[104]

When the preacher tells his[her] story and "tells the story" of biblical young people whom God called to service, it will "inspire" listeners to their part in the story and move them to have the "courage" to affirm their place of service in their context.

The Courage to Be a Servant

The task of the "story sermon" is to testify to the hearer the ***courage*** to affirm themselves and others "in spite of" the threat of nonbeing.[105] The sermon is to engender courage — the power to live creatively to bring "transforming reality" to situations that experience "the anxiety of meaninglessness," the "anxiety of loss," and the "loss of a spiritual center."[106] Preaching the idea of the hero activates psychologically each hearer to consider "service" and/or bringing "social transformation" into life at some point or at some time in their life.

The claim of the narrative story is to speak to the "depth dimension" of the young adult's life to engender the courage to go beneath the "shallowness" of their lives "to penetrate below the surfaces in order to learn what things

---

[104] King, *Strength to Love*, 114.
[105] Tillich, *Courage to Be*, 43.
[106] Ibid., 46 – 47.

really are"[107] and to affect them positively. In going to the "depth" of life, Charles Cosgrove and W. Dow Edgerton observe that preaching "the story" reconstructs our world. We are moved from the cognitive to the imaginative. We visualize alternative worlds that move us to the dynamic aspects of life. The imagery of the narrative story touches "the depths" and then stirs the "surface" of our lives.[108]

Tillich affirms that the text, the story, solicits us to descend to the "depth of life" thus freeing us from the routine of life. It pushes us to face the hazards of life both good and bad. It causes us to "move forward." We are shaken by the earthquake of the narrative story, and it "disrupts our self knowledge, that we are willing to look into a deeper level of our being."[109]

It is my contention that preaching the narrative story of the hero pushes us to the "depths," beyond the "surface," beyond the "routine" to a "deeper level" of our existence, thus giving us the "courage" to see an "alternative" to the "threats" of life that come against us and keep us stuck. Tillich asserts that preaching the narrative story of the hero gives the listener the courage to face their "anxiety," "fear," and the "threat of nonbeing."[110]

---

[107] Paul Tillich, "The Depth of Existence," *The Shaking of the Foundations* (New York, NY: Charles Scribner's Sons, 1948), 52 – 53/

[108] Charles Cosgrove and W. Dow Edgerton, *In Other Words: Incarnational Translation for Preaching* (Grand Rapids, MI: William B. Eerdmans Publishing Company, 2007), 18 – 19.

[109] Cosgrove and Edgerton, 55 – 56.

[110] Tillich, *Courage*, 78.

One narrative story that illustrates ***courage and service*** was presented in the sermon, "You Can Be a Hero Too!" (1 Samuel 17:30 – 40).[111] King Saul and the army of Israel were faced with a ***power*** "threat" in the giant Goliath. To face this threat, David presented himself to King Saul as "your servant." David ***received the courage*** to face the giant Goliath as he reflected his past experience and "story" as a shepherd facing lions and bears that were threats to his sheepfold. In his conversation with King Saul, David named the Lord God as the power that was greater than Goliath and with God's power, the giant could be faced and overcome.

Charles Campbell further explicates that social transformation begins when we identify, name, and realize what and who the giants (Goliaths) and ***principalities (archai)*** are in our context. We access courage when we accept the ***powers (exousia)*** of the Lord God are greater than the Goliaths in our context.

The ***powers in scripture***, according to Campbell, are multiple. They are superhuman creatures with a spirit and life of their own, beyond the control of human beings. They are aggressive actors in the world, shaping human life in profound ways. Not simply personal, spiritual beings 'up in the heavens' somewhere, the powers are embodied and active in concrete, structural realities.[112]

---

[111]   This sermon was preached November 2005.

[112]   Charles Campbell, *The Word Before the Powers: An Ethic of Preaching* (Louisville, KY: Westminster John Knox Press, 2002), 10.

The powers interact with each other and blend with one another, in the text of scripture, until the reader of the text is overwhelmed by the torrent of powers such as *authorities, rulers, thrones, spirits, demons, serpents, dragons, lions, beasts, Satan, and the Devil.*[113] The result of these interactions is "chaos, as the rival powers struggle for survival and dominance."[114] ***The powers***, whether spiritual or social reality, are "at work in and through concrete, material institutions, structures, and systems in the world. This is how the powers shape the lives of most of the people to whom [we] preach."[115]

The recognition of our need to confront ***the institutional and structural powers*** "entices us with the allure of heroism."[116] Because of our ***heroic consciousness***, we long to face the ***demonic structural powers*** in our context. To face the powers, we must ask, "How does Jesus ***transform/redeem/overcome*** the negative powers in the narrative story? and "How can I assist in transforming the powers that are opposed to dignity, liberty, justice, and equality in the narrative story and my personal story?

David's story demonstrated the courage of "self-affirmation." David believed the Lord was with Him to insure the "preservation"[117] of others. He presented himself before the power of Goliath, with the power of God, to overcome what threatened him and others. He was

---

[113] Campbell, *The Word,* 13.

[114] Ibid., 11.

[115] Ibid., 15.

[116] Hedges, 83.

[117] Tillich, *Courage,* 78.

victorious in transforming the situation of fear, loss, and meaninglessness. [118]

What then is "the courage of the hero" in the preached narrative story? The hero's courage is to serve and to bring social transformation that can be defined as "the readiness to take upon oneself negatives, . . . , for the sake of a fuller positivity. Without this self-affirmation life could not be preserved or increased."[119] Young adults are requisitioned through story preaching to face the negatives, in their context, with a hope of bringing a positive to life, to preserve life, and to increase it.

Within my local church context, since my arrival in August of 1999, young adults have not been successful in finding a "place" within the walls of our congregational life. Most young people who participated in church ministry in some form have struggled not to be pigeon-holed into a particular way of offering service and social transformation to their context. In the story of David and Goliath, David broke out of the King Saul's prescribed way to bring social transformation. David, at first put on King Saul's armor to fight Goliath and then pulled it off. David chose to use what he was familiar with – a sling and smooth stones. It was David's desire to "be of service" in the area of his giftedness. He became *a partner* with King Saul in service and social transformation.[120]

---

[118] Tillich, *Courage,* 20, 26 – 27, 46 – 47.

[119] Ibid.

[120] Jack Skiles reflection on partnership of young adults in the church ministry and service, August 28, 2007.

The Courage to Be a Social Transformer

Social transformation is the process whereby the "activity of the demonic powers in the world"[121] are contained, restrained, and restructured to bring life to what was once dead, disorganized, and disoriented. Social transformation asks how can we give "attention to the legion of powers that oppress people and hold them captive"?[122] Social transformation takes place when we aggressively begin in small or large ways to reshape the structural realities that have held us captive, that have made us feel trapped, and have left us to feel powerless.[123]

The contention of social transformation is "something can change." We do not have to be "swept along by forces beyond [our] control."[124] We can make a difference. Preaching the story invigorates young adults to respond to the biblical vision to "make" and "be" the difference in their worlds through service and social transformation.

The story sermon aim is to incite the hero to become *a social transformer* who leads people to grow through challenge, dialogue, and the exchange of ideas "to enlighten the world" and to "affirm the deepest level of truth about it"[125] and God. In ***Luke 4:16 - 20***, the Lord Jesus Christ put Himself in the prophet Isaiah's story of the "God's Deliverer" who preaches, delivers, and sets free the captives and those

---

[121] Campbell, *The Word Before the Powers*, 6.
[122] Ibid., 7.
[123] Ibid., 10.
[124] Ibid., 6.
[125] Pearson, *Hero*, 90, 91, 125.

who are bruised. The Lord Jesus' ***biblical foundation*** (Isaiah 62:2) for ***social transformation*** affirmed ***the hero within*** Himself to preach to the poor, to heal the broken, to preach deliverance to captives, to help the blind recover their sight, and to set free the bruised, by His preaching that the grace of God operates within our social context in spite of what keeps us stuck and constricted.

Through this narrative story (Luke 4:16 – 19; Isaiah 62:2), we learn that the Lord Jesus was "grasped" by the Spirit for a "humane concern" based on historical biblical and theological foundations. In the story, just as the Lord Jesus risked listening to God, young adults are called to "risk listening to the divine voice"[126] and become serviceable transformative agents in their context.

The ***contextual formation*** of the story narrative must become a contemporary, "right now" story. The "story" can help the listener to see the problems and conflicts in the text, and the conflicts and problems in their personal context. The narrative story summons the hearer to ***be heroic*** by ***taking responsibility*** in their existential situation of "stuckness," thus becoming the ***solution*** and resolution of the problems and conflicts they and others face. The hero, in any story narrative, is the person who is both responsible[127] and responsive to get people going again.

---

[126] Clader, *Voicing the Vision* (New York, NY: Morehouse Publishing, 2003), 13.

[127] Campbell, *Hero*, 45.

The Hero as Social Transformer

Why preach on the biblical theology of heroism for social transformation? The hero is a life giver. This is a person who cares for and sustains the life of others with hope.[128] The hero is "generative," a "creative life force [who is] . . . concerned about the rights, safety, [and] health . . . of all human beings."[129] The hero "is a protector of the weak and disempowered. S/he does what is necessary "to assure justice and equality of opportunity for all people."[130] The hero is a "transformer" who uses their "creative life force" to empower others.[131]

Within certain biblical stories, there have been persons who have been heroic; their heroism changed social structures that hindered peoples' lives. King Josiah, a young adult, in 2 Kings 22 listened to the words of Huldah the prophetess to bring "social transformation" and revival to the nation of Judah. In her challenge to King Josiah, he becomes heroic in that he took responsibility and responded to the spiritual, emotional, political, and economic needs of his nation. He was heroic in that he cared for and was committed to the well being of others.[132]

Telling the narrative story of heroic actions is a way to stir young adults to "image" and "visualize" what they

---

[128] Robert Moore and Douglas Gillette, *The King Within: Accessing the King in the Male Psyche* (New York, NY: Avon Books, 1992), 149.

[129] Moore and Gillette, *King Within*, 153.

[130] Ibid.

[131] Ibid., 156.

[132] Pearson, *Hero*, 111, 105, 104, 103, 109.

can do in the area of service; heroic stories can supply the stimulus to permit them to claim their place of transformative service "within" or "outside" the organized structure of the church institution in order to assist people in their crisis and trauma,[133] and to influence them to go on with life[134] in spite of their experiences of powerlessness, pain, loneliness, and fear.[135]

---

[133]   Robert Moore and Douglas Gillette, *The Magician Within: Accessing the Shaman in the Male Psyche* (New York, NY: William Morrow and Company, Inc., 1993), 117, 119, 120, 121.

[134] Pearson, *Hero*, 44, 42, 150.

[135] Ibid., 82.

Four

The Project and its Rationale: The Method of Shaping the Story

In *The Art of Biblical Narrative,* Alter asserts that "biblical authors [were] . . . urgently conscious of telling a story in order to reveal the imperative truth of God's works in history."[136] The preacher should have an "imperative" to present the ***preaching narrative stories of heroic action*** with the aim of stirring the imagination and consciousness of young adult listeners to be participants in the ongoing mission of God's saving purposes in the context of their lives. The "story" method of preaching attempts to give young adults, who are limited in their biblical knowledge, a way to be informed, inspired, and engaged in systematic bible study and analysis that can be transferred into the analysis of their own lives and the experiences of others.

---

[136] Alter, *Biblical Narrative,* 46.

Narrative Preaching as a Method to Assist in Discovering Ones Identity and Vocation

Telling the story through narrative preaching intends to reveal the processes whereby young people can begin their **search for identity and vocation**. In **Genesis 46:2**, Jacob received the call from God to be a great nation. **Exodus 3:4** reveals Moses' call to be a deliverer. **1 Samuel 3:4** sights the call of young Samuel to fill the priestly – prophetic service of Eli. **Jeremiah 3:4 - 6** affirms Jeremiah's call as a youth to speak to the nations. **1 Samuel 16:12 – 13** declares young David's anointing to be the second king of Israel. **Isaiah 6:8** shares Isaiah's call to prophetic ministry.

The aim of the narrative story is to reveal a "narrative theology" that asserts that young adults are included in "a grand plot: God is reconciling the world . . ."[137] Telling the story through narrative preaching is "the method of inviting [young adult] generations to participate in the **"mega story"** of God, to discover their identity within that Story, and to develop a character in light of that identity."[138]

As to developing "personal meaning," narrative preaching enables young adults to examine the "cause and effect" of peoples lives, as well as the consequences. It allows them, with imagination, to interact with people in the text and

---

[137] Jim Hampton and Rick Edwards, *Worship Centered Teaching: Guiding Youth to Discover their Identity in Christ* (Kansas City, MO: Word Action Publishing Company, 2001), 26.
[138] Ibid.

weave meaning into their lives, thus gaining illumination and significance for their situational moments.[139]

Through story preaching young adults can assess how persons in the biblical text gained a sense of identity and personhood. Who nurtured them? Who were the persons responsible for their maturation or lack of it? Lee Butler, Jr. asserts that identity formation takes place in the encounter of others like us. As we acknowledge, relate to, and identify with others, our identity and personhood is being formed and reformed.[140]

Identity is predicated on *social location.* The narrative story allows young people to examine the position and place of characters in the text. It offers them a vision of their place and position in the social context of their work, home, church, and community?[141] Hearing the biblical story gives young adults a biblical and theological foundation to examine how those in the text gained their point of orientation and purpose.[142]

Narrative preaching can assist young adults in assessing their *role in the culture.* Role is "what I do," [and] my social responsibility.[143] Within the biblical narratives, we observe people whose role was liberation and salvation.[144]

---

[139] Lee H. Butler, Jr., *Liberating Our Dignity Saving our Souls* (St. Louis, MO: Chalice Press, 2006), 27.

[140] Ibid., 4.

[141] Ibid., viii.

[142] Ibid., xi.

[143] Ibid., 4.

[144] Ibid., vii.

As young adults examine the biblical past, they connect with Israel's past and Israel's great faith identity.

Young adults who read the biblical texts are connected with their ***African past***[145] in the Bible. To understand who they are, young adults must connect with their African motherland to understand its history and spirituality, thus not being ashamed of who they are historically and contextually. Telling the story of their biblical African past will show how African people contributed to salvation history that was powerful and liberating.

While preaching the narrative story, the preacher should make contextual and visible the story of young adults' heroic mission in their ***American present.***[146] Individuals, such as, Dr. Martin Luther King, Jr., Julian Bond, Fred Shuttlesworth, Rosa Parks, A. Phillip Randolph, Emmett Till, Rev. Jesse L. Jackson, Sr., Rev. Al Sharpton, Rev. Paul Jakes, Jr. and a host of others in our American past and present were young adults who served as social transformers. Their attempts were to ***resist*** and ***transform*** the constructs that are opposed to dignity, privilege, liberty, justice, survival, and equality.[147]

Preaching "the story" has as its aim to be ***"transformational."***[148] Telling the story can "evoke a new orientation" in the experience and the imagination of the listener to help them through the crisis or complication in

---

[145] Butler, 11.
[146] Ibid., 8.
[147] Ibid.
[148] Ibid., 31.

their own experience or personal story. In each situation of "telling the stories" of Ruth, young Samuel, and the lost son, young adults have been presented with crisis of loss, death, and trauma. The "story" holds up to the listener "an encounter" and a "revelation"[149] of how to meet the upheavals in their lives. In each encounter with the story, we are formed, reformed, and redefined in our identity.[150] Through "the story," young adults can possibly gain a growing edge in determining their self-concept, identity[151] and destination in the context of their own personal stories and experiences.

Preaching the story of "heroic action" aims to enable young people to understand how they have been *heroic*, and how they can become heroic. To aid young people in finding their social location of service, ask the following:

1. *Theologically*: What God is doing in my context?[152]

2. *Sociologically*: How do I understand my *role in the culture?*[153]

3. *Biblically*: What are my biblical foundations that call me to participate in social transformation activities?

4. How can I be used by God to help others through their *crisis*?

---

[149] Lowry, *The Sermon*, 29.
[150] Butler, 9.
[151] Ibid.
[152] Ibid., viii.
[153] Clader, 4.

The Conclusions and Results of the Methodology: How to Tell the Story

The significance the "story sermon" offers to the imagination of the hearer are **ways they can be serviceable** in the world. "Telling of the story" elevates the listener's consciousness to participate in the work of God "in" and "beyond" their context. The preacher, when telling the narrative story, "inspires [listeners] to achieve the fullness of [their] being."[154] As you are "raised on a dais"[155] you give the listener "the capacity to differentiate one thing from another and to make value distinctions between them."[156] You offer words to the listener that gives them "discernment" and you help them to "cut through confusion."[157] You hold the word of *"gnosis"* (knowledge) that helps people "distinguish between light and darkness, good and evil."[158] Your preaching is "life – enhancing rather than death – dealing."[159]

The preacher's words are *"generative"* – you are a life – giver. Through your preaching, you are "always saying 'yes' to life, 'yes' to the new, 'yes' to creativity./ [You] thrust [forth] the divine urge to penetrate the profane and seed it

---

[154] Moore and Gillette, *The King Within*, 121.
[155] Ibid., 124.
[156] Ibid., 141.
[157] Ibid.
[158] Ibid.
[159] Ibid., 125.

with the sacred."[160] As you preach, you in fact impart the eternal into the lives of the listeners.[161]

---

[160] Moore and Gillette, *King Within,* 126.
[161] Ibid., 129.

Jive
The Significance for the Wider Audience

The Preacher as Hero

In the beginning of this ministry project on "Preaching to young adults to encourage them toward Heroic Action," the question was asked, by Dr. Craig Satterlee,[162] why did I want to engage in such a study? My answer was, "I wanted to be a hero!" Since that time, I have come to realize that the "preacher is a hero too." By definition, a hero is a person who **gets others unstuck** from their predicament, but also a hero is a person who gets persons **unstuck from "limited thinking**."[163] The preacher's goal is to get listeners "unstuck" from both "existential thinking" and their "existential situations" to get them moving again.

---

[162] Craig Satterlee is the Dean of the Doctor of Ministry Program in Preaching, Lutheran School of Theology, Chicago, IL. This question was asked during the Colloquy 2 Class as we were refining our Thesis Proposal, Summer, 2006.

[163] John C. Maxwell, *Thinking For A Change* (New York, NY: Center Street, 2003), 3 – 5.

The preacher is a hero, in that through the exposition of the text, [s]he "expands" the vision of the hearer, and opens them to "alternatives" and "options" for living.

Moore and Gillette have observed within ***developmental psychology***, young people need a "constitutive glance." They need someone to "see" them. They need someone to "touch" them. The "seeing" and the "touching" consolidates and validates their identity. When you, as the preacher, focus your preaching toward young people, you in fact, are heroic in that you "see them" and "embrace them."[164] Efrem Smith adds, "Raising up young heroes for God begins with seeing youth as young heroes from the first moment you lay eyes on them."[165] We must begin "seeing in young people what they can't see in themselves. . ./ that God can use them to do great things."[166]

The Heroic Aspects of the Spoken Word

As preacher, when you "tell the story," you offer young people a ***"spoken blessing"*** that points to their value; it offers them a picture of their future, and it demonstrates your commitment to help them realize God's future for their lives.[167] When you speak the word, it brings ***light*** to young people's uncertainty, ***freedom*** from their oppression, ***liberation and justice*** for their lives, a new ***identity***, and it offers ***direction*** for their lives.[168]   You must preach

[164] Moore and Gillette, *King Within*, 129.
[165] Smith, *Raising Up Young Heroes*, 23.
[166] Smith, *Heroes*, 26.
[167] Moore and Gillette, *King Within*, 130.
[168] Smith, *Heroes*, 28 – 29.

so that young people can "hear words of affirmation, encouragement and love. Words are powerful. They make an impact on our lives."[169]

Two Young Adults and Their Heroic Actions
Marquelle: Service

After the September 2006 sermon, "Somebody's Calling Your Name," Marquelle, a young adult man came to me and purported that he did not know what God wanted to do with his life. He desired to do something to help the church, but did not know what gifts he had to offer or where he could be of use. I told him that I could not give him an assignment. He would have to listen to what God was saying through the sermon, through Bible studies, and through trying out different things that he had an interest in.

After doing these things, I told him to stay in prayer and trust the Lord to reveal what he was to do. What did Marquelle do?

o   He started an evening basketball game for
    about five young adult men on Wednesday
    nights.
o   Through outreach initiatives, two years later,
    he recruited over 50 young adult men who are
    now organized into a basketball league.
o   Marquelle's actions have been heroic in that
    he has established a service ministry "in"

---

[169] Smith, *Heroes*, 27.

the church building to those who are on the "outside."

o His approach to these young men has been what he calls a "non – threatening witness."

o He feels that this program has offered young adult men the following – "a league of their own," a place of fellowship, clean competition, sportsmanship, mentorship, and discipline.

Paul: Social Transformation

In the fall of 2005 and the winter of 2006, a series of sermons were preached on "Somebody's Calling Your Name" and "You Can Be a Hero Too!" to inspire young adults toward the idea of heroic action that would lead to social transformation. One young adult man in the congregation came to me and shared that the sermons encouraged him to fulfill his lifelong dream to engage in political and social action.

Paul, from the time he was fifteen years old, told me that he wanted to be the Mayor of Chicago. He felt that the 2006 Aldermanic race was the right time to take leadership in a Chicago ward where he lived. He expressed that his purpose for seeking the aldermanic position was to "minister" to the community. His political talk sounded more like "church" talk. He wanted to bring "revival" to the community. What did he do?

o During his campaign, he held several prayer meetings and unity rallies with other candidates in the ward.

o His aim was to develop a platform that would give vision and vitality to people.

o He held about three rallies where ministers in the ward were invited to preach to bring "unity" to the ward.

o His idea of revival was twofold – He wanted to make better the schools, the recreational facilities, and the streets where children could play safely.

Though Paul did not win the aldermanic position, he continues to do the following:

o He meets monthly with his campaign workers for prayer and strategy at our church for social change.

o He assists the alderman elect to help benefit the ward with its many systemic problems. As issues arise, his team seeks to develop action plans to meet these challenges.[170]

Paul's story is an illustration of heroic action that is serviceable and socially transforming to both those "inside" and "outside" of the church.

---

[170] Interview with Paul, Saturday, June 30, 2007, as it relates to heroic social transformative action, in response to the sermon series "Somebody is Calling My Name" and "You Can Be a Hero Too!"

Six

Conclusion: The Preacher and the Preaching Task

This initiative on *preaching to awaken the hero in young adults* is aimed at addressing helping young adults find their purpose and place in congregational ministry. During this initiative on narrative preaching, it has been suggested that the biblical narrative stories hold the key to "identity and vocation."

The Preacher's Task: Heroism through Personal Relationship

In beginning this preaching project, Dr. Jack Skiles[171] discussed with me reasons young adults don't listen seriously to the preacher. A key insight was the preacher's lack of *personal interaction* with them. A "hero" does not live in isolation from people. The preacher becomes a hero when [s]he has *personal contact* with young people and allows them to "share their story" with the preacher.

---

[171] Dr. Jack Skiles is my advisor and preaching mentor in the Doctor of Ministry in Preaching program (McCormick Theological Seminary, Chicago, IL) from June 2005 to May 2008.

What sometimes follows is – young people will hear "the preacher's story."

Hampton and Edwards have asked, "How are we to pass the ancient faith to the next generation?"[172] They suggest that like a baton, we must recite God's story (Deuteronomy 6:7 – 9) by "recounting the amazing exploits and sincere faith of [our] ancestors."[173] This is done as we walk with them down the road. We must "tell the story" from the pulpit and from where they stand to ". . . creatively invite the next generation to become active participants in God's ongoing activity . . ."[174]

How do we **walk with young people** so that our preaching can awaken the hero within them? The preacher needs to **enter the story of young people**. To make valid the biblical stories of relationship, the preacher should begin modeling "relational" interactions and "personal" engagement with young adults that will give them a vision of viable relational actions to pursue. ***To hear and engage with young people,*** Mary Mulligan et al. suggest the following:

1. Young people need to feel "one with" the preacher.[175]

---

[172] Hampton and Edwards, *Worship*, 24.

[173] Ibid..

[174] Ibid.

[175] Mary Mulligan, Diane Turner – Sharazz, Dawn Wilelm, and Ronald Allen, *Believing in Preaching* (St. Louis, MO: Chalice Press, 2005), 68.

2. Connect ***within the walls of the church*** by involving young adults in leadership roles and the story of the church.[176]
3. Connect with young adults on committees, sharing with them in church programs and events, and special "inside" church projects.
4. Stand alongside of young adults[177] in outside activities – casual meals, ball games, school events, college activities, and neighborhood events.[178]

To assist young people in assuming leadership roles of service "in" and "beyond" the church," the following are valuable assessments –

1. Establish a leadership friendly atmosphere.
2. Communicate to young adults that they are needed.
3. Develop and communicate opportunities of service and leadership to those who feel led to participate.
4. Allow the service and leadership of young adults to evolve based on their creativity and giftedness.

---

[176] Four young people are serving in the following Church functions: First Vice President of the Emmanuel Christian School Board, The Director of the Emmanuel Christian School Alumni Association, Captain of our January Calendar Circle Leadership and another is serving as Captain of the Nurses Health Unit of the church. This is an extraordinary leap in giving young adults leadership in our Church and Christian School structure.

[177] Mulligan et all, *Believing*, 68.

[178] Ibid.

The Preaching Task

The task of telling God's story is to allow young adults to **see what God has done** in the lives of biblical young people and how God can use them in "unexpected" "unanticipated" ways. By preaching the biblical story, the preacher gives young people a biblical vision that will enable them to explore their possibilities and potentials. The preacher should do the following:

o Preach the "narrative story" as the young adult's story of God's word "to" and "for" them.

o Be **proactive** in preaching to move young people to have "compassion and justice."[179]

o Help young people realize they can have a future impact.[180]

o Encourage faith in young people to make a radical difference not only in their own lives but also in the lives of those around them."[181]

The preacher must continue to help young adults hear and respond to the gospel story that calls them to mission, service, and social transformation. "Telling the story" over and over again in creative ways can help young people think about themselves, and how they feel about themselves. It is hoped that through "telling the story" that young people will change how they think about themselves, thus bringing

---

[179] Smith, *Heroes*, 11.
[180] Ibid., 17.
[181] Ibid., 26.

about a change in their actions,[182] thus bringing a change in their lives that will send them on their journey to transform their world.

[182] Maxwell, *Thinking for a Change*, 5.

Bibliography

Allen, Ronald. *The Preaching and Practical Ministry*. St. Louis, MO: Chalice, 2001.

Alter, David. *The Art of Biblical Narrative*. Berkeley, CA: Basic Books, 1981.

Barna, George. *The Power of Vision*. Ventura, CA: Regal Books, 2003.

Bonem, Mike and Patterson, Roger. *Leading From the Second Chair: Serving Your Church, Fulfilling Your Role, and Realizing Your Dreams*. San Francisco, CA: A Wiley Imprint, 2005.

Brewer, H. Michael. *Who Needs a Superhero? Finding Virtue, Vice, and What's Holy in the Comics*. Grand Rapids, MI: Baker Books, 2004.

Bromiley, Geoffrey. *Theological Dictionary of the New Testament*. Grand Rapids, MI: William B. Eerdmans Publishing Company, 1985.

Butler, Lee H. *Liberating Our Dignity Saving our Souls*. St. Louis, MO: Chalice Press, 2006.

Campbell, Charles. *The Word Before the Powers: An Ethic of Preaching.* Louisville, KY: Westminster John Knox Press, 2002.

Campbell, Joseph. *The Hero with a Thousand Faces.* Princeton, NJ: Princeton University Press, 1949.

Clader, Linda. *Voicing the Vision.* Harrisburg, PA: Morehouse Publishing, 2003.

Connors, Roger, Smith, Tome and Hickman, Craig. *The Oz Principle.* New York, NY: The Penguin Group, 2004.

Cosgrove, Charles and Edgerton, W. Dow. *In Other Words: Incarnational Translation for Preaching.* Grand Rapids, MI: William B. Eerdmans Publishing Company, 2007.

Dean, Kenda. *Practicing Passion: Youth and the Quest for a Passionate Church.* Grand Rapids, MI: William B. Eerdmans Publishing Company, 2004.

Dickens, Charles "A Tale of Two Cities," accessed 2 November 2007, <http://www.quotationspage.com/quotes/Charles_Dickens.html>.

Erik Erikson. *Childhood and Society.* New York, NY: W. W. Norton and Company, 1963.

_____. *Identity: Youth and Crisis.* New York, NY: W. W. Norton and Company, 1968.

_____. *The Life Cycle Completed.* New York, NY: W. W. Norton and Company, 1982.

Fields, Doug. *Purpose Driven Youth Ministry*. Grand Rapids, MI: Zondervan Publishing House, 1998.

Fosdick, Harry E. "What Is the Matter with Preaching," In Mike Graves (ed.), *What's the Matter with Preaching Today?* (Louisville, KY: Westminster John Knox Press, 2004.

Goldingay, John. *Models for Interpretation of Scripture*. Grand Rapids, MI: William B. Eerdmans Publishing Company, 1995.

Graves, Mike (ed.). *What's the Matter with Preaching Today?* Louisville, KY: Westminster John Knox Press, 2004.

Gross, Larry. "Bears Star Wants to Help Sack Crime in City," *Chicago Defender,* 29 – 30 October 2007, 24.

Hampton, Jim and Edwards, Rick. *Worship Centered Teaching: Guiding Youth to Discover their Identity in Christ*. Kansas City, MO: Word Action Publishing Company, 2001.

Hedges, Chris. *War Is a Force That Gives Us Meaning.* New York, NY: Anchor Books, 2002

Hybels, Bill. *Holy Discontent: Fueling the Fire that Ignites Personal Vision*. Grand Rapids, MI: Zondervan, 2007.

King, Martin Luther. *Strength to Love*. Philadelphia, PA: Fortress Press, 1963.

Larsen, David. *Telling the Old, Old Story: The Art of Narrative Preaching*. Grand Rapids, MI: Kregel Publications, 1995.

Long, Thomas, "No News is Bad News," In Mike Graves (ed.), *What's the Matter with Preaching Today?* Louisville, KY: Westminster John Knox Press, 2004.

Lowry, Eugene. *The Homiletical Plot: The Sermon as Narrative Art Form.* Louisville, KY: Westminster John Knox Press, 2001.

_____ . *The Sermon: Dancing the Edge of Mystery.* Nashville, TN: Abingdon Press, 1997.

Maxwell, John C. *Thinking For A Change.* New York, NY: Center Street, 2003.

Moore, Robert and Gillette, Douglas. *The King Within: Accessing the King in the Male Psyche.* New York, NY: Avon Books, 1992.

_____ . *The Warrior Within: Accessing the Knight in the Male Psyche.* New York, NY: William Morrow and Company, Inc., 1992.

Mulligan, Mary, Turner – Sharazz, Diane, Wilhelm, Dawn, and Allen, Ronald. *Believing in Preaching.* St. Louis, MO: Chalice Press, 2005.

Partible, Leo in H. Michael Brewer, *Who Needs a Superhero? Finding Virtue, Vice, and What's Holy in the Comics.* Grand Rapids, MI: Baker Books, 2004.

Pearson, Carol. *Awakening the Heroes Within.* New York, NY: Harper Collins Publishers, 1991.

_____ . *The Hero Within.* New York, NY: Harper Collins Publishers, 1989.

Saunders, Stanley and Campbell, Charles. *The Word on the Street: Performing Scriptures in the Urban Context.* Grand Rapids, MI: William B. Eerdmans Publishing Company, 2002.

Siris: The Ethics of Superheroes, (08 July 2004) <http://branemrys.blogspot.com/2004/07/ethics-of-superheroes.html>. Accessed 21 July 2007.

Skiles, Jack, (26 August 2007). "Courage to Stand Tall,"<http://www.firstunitedchurchbloomington.org/sundayworship/sermon_new.html> Accessed 1 September 2007.

Smith, Efrem. *Raising Up Young Heroes: Developing a Revolutionary Youth Ministry.* Downers Grove, IL: Intervarsity Press, 2004.

Stanley, Andy et. al. *Seven Practices of Practical Ministry.* Sisters, OR: Multnomah Publishers, 2004.

Thomas, Frank. *They Like To Never Quit Praisin' God.* Cleveland, OH: United Church Press, 1997.

Tillich, Paul. *Systematic Theology: Three Volumes in One.* Chicago, IL: The University of Chicago Press, 1967.

Tillich, Paul. "You are Accepted." *The Shaking of the Foundations.* New York, NY: Charles Scribner's Sons, 1948.

_____ . *The Courage to Be.* New Haven, CT: Yale University Press, 1952.

_____ . *The Shaking of the Foundations.* New York, NY: Charles Scribner's Sons, 1948.

Washington, Denzel. *A Hand to Guide Me.* Des Moines, IA: Meredith Books, 2006.

Zodhiates, Spiros. *The Complete Word Study Dictionary: New Testament.* Chattanooga, TN: AMG Publishers, 1992.

Appendix A:
Church Location

This thesis project is located in a small African American congregation on the southwest side of Chicago in the Auburn Gresham community. The church moved to the corner of 8301 S. Damen Avenue, Chicago, Illinois in January 1974 following its organization in January 1973. For almost one year, the church worshiped in the Morgan Park High School before purchasing its present location.

The community to which the Emmanuel family relocated was in transition in the mid 1970s. The church is located in the 18th Ward of Chicago and is in a section of the ward that is predominately Black. The church's major boundaries are bordered by 79th Street to the north, Ashland Avenue to the west, 87th Street to the north, and Western Avenue to the west. The housing in the community is about 60 years old and is selling at an average of $150 - 180,000 dollars.

Since the church's organization over 35 years ago, the church has become a predominate congregation of senior adults who have supported and given their energies to the church over the three decades of the church's ministry. In the height of the church's beginning she would serve nearly six-hundred worshippers weekly. At present, the attendance averages about two hundred and fifty weekly.

At present our congregation has as active members about ***125 senior adults*** from 65 years to 92 years, roughly ***75 median adults*** from 36 – 64, and ***15 young adults*** from 19 – 35 and ***about 35 children and youth*** from preschool to high school status. With the shrinking young adult congregation and the ***death rate*** of our senior adult members our congregation will be on the brink of losing a generation to carry on the church's mission and work.

The following are observations that have led to the loss of young adults in our congregation over the years:

A. When the anchor senior adult dies, the young adults in the family leave church.

B. Young adults who marry usually attend the church of their spouse.

C. Young adults who grew up in the church join other churches to establish their own identity away from their parents in the congregation.

D. Upon high school graduation, as young adults, their parents cannot "make" them attend.

E. College bound young adults leave and remain in the area of relocation.

F. Some are consumed with careers and new families, not church work.

Other young people are looking for "up beat" worship styles that attend to their generational experience.

Appendix B:
Reflections from the Preaching Peer Group[183]

Since September 2005, Pastor Jackson has grown as a preacher. The following statements are reflections on his growth and development as a preacher and his focus on Young Adult service and ministry. To capture the attention of young adults, Pastor Jackson has become more animated than usual as he has attempted to portray heroic persons and their behavior in the text preached to young adults. He stated that a course in "Preaching as Performance" helped him to realize that there is a bit of drama and theater in preaching. Preaching is not a lecture; it is interaction, movement and voice. It is a call to hearers to be participants in the drama of the narrative story. Pastor Jackson is declaring the word of God with much wit and imagination.

He uses illustrations of current and old television programs and movies to capture the attention of all the

_____
[183] Summative reflections on the Pastor Jackson's growth since being in the Preaching Program by the Preaching Peer Group (William Wyatt, Mary McElroy, Albert Johnson, Elston Green, Ricord Jackson, Donald Williams) since the Summer 2005 to the present.

listeners. He is able to connect and correlate the experience of the illustrations into the lives of the young adult listeners and is able to help them make application from the illustration to their lives. Pastor Jackson is speaking more to the conscience of the hearers. By doing that, he proves to not be judgmental of anyone, recognizing that everyone has yet to come to the hero's' status of their lives.

Second, it is evident that there has been research done in the text to be preached. Pastor Jackson is using more references being made to current events and connecting more to the congregation on a more personal level. He injects more humor into his sermon to get his point across. His messages are coming across "more fiery" perhaps than some of his previous messages.

The insights that have been gained in explaining the narrative story has begun to motivate and hold the interest of the congregation and young adult hearers. He is being precise in his message as to its purpose and its call to young people to listen to the voice of God and respond. He has gained better ways of making the message relevant and how using words that "talk to," instead of "above the head" of the congregants.

Third, Pastor Jackson is gaining methodology as to how to preach ***inter-generationally*** to a mixed audience. He is moving from a more complicated analysis of scripture to one where the sermon can be understood on an everyday life experience. He has begun to break the sermon down for everyone to understand. He is becoming a man of thought. He is becoming a well rounded pastor who is able to interject into his written sermons the top news story of the day that needs a Christian witness.

Four, the inclusion of youth and young adults, in helping him give understanding to the text, has been a great help to get their view point inserted into the sermon. He is gaining insight as to ways to motivate and capture the interest of young people. He is gaining a greater awareness of what young people want to hear.

We have been challenged to continue to help the pastor in sermon preparation through input and prayer. We have grown personally in God's word to help young adults grow toward their mission. We have been stimulated by the Pastor's preaching to live our lives according to the purpose of God. He has preached that we mean something to God. God interacts with each of us personally because God wants to work in our lives for the good of others.

Appendix C:
Developing the Sermon Purpose

The **sermon purpose** defines what the sermon is to do in this particular preaching event.

In view of *the many people who are stuck in a crisis of need*, I want to help the congregants to *become aware and know persons who can "do something" to get them unstuck in crisis situations*. The call is *acknowledge our crisis needs and take actions to engage them our entire lives*. I will achieve this by means of *telling a story narrative that leads us to 1) be aware of personal crisis needs, 2) acknowledge and identify the cause of the crisis needs and 3) to take actions to get unstuck from the crisis needs on a continuous basis*.

Part 1: The situation – Describe the concern, issue or need that brings the sermon to this particular place and time and the biblical text chosen for the occasion.

Part 2: The goal – As a result of the need, what should the people experience to meet the needs, issues and concerns?

Part 3: The means – Describe how and by what biblical literary form the hearers will be led into this experience and outcome.

Appendix D:
Pre – Questionnaire:
Interpreting the Bible Story

1. Write in two sentences what you believe the *scripture's purpose* is for your life.

2. Write the *conflict, or the struggle*, the main character is facing in the biblical situation.[184]

3. List the *possible solutions* that the scripture is offering to answer the problem and conflict in the passage.

---

[184] Jack Seymour, Margaret Crain, and Joseph Crockett, *Educating Christians: The Intersection of Meaning, Learning, and Vocation* (Nashville, TN: Abingdon Press, 1993),

4. Write the ***insights and new possibilities*** you see in the passage for your life.

5. Write the "Aha!," ***the answer*** you see to the problem and conflict in the story.

6. Write the ***future possibility*** that scripture is calling you to move toward.

Appendix E:
Post-questionnaire following sermon

1. As a result of the sermon, describe what you are looking and questing for now.

2. Briefly describe what God is calling you to do or become.

3. What *new vision* did the sermon offer for your journey?

4. As a result of the sermon, what is God calling you to do now?

Appendix F:
Pre – Post questionnaire:
Understanding God's Call

Pre-questionnaire before sermon

1. State the personal quest or journey you are on presently.

2. Describe briefly who you are becoming as a result of your journey.

3. What is the vision (What God wants for my life) you have for your journey?

4. Describe your present personal mission (What you are to do with your life now).

Post-questionnaire following sermon

1. As a result of the sermon, describe what you are looking and questing for now.

2. Briefly describe what God through the sermon is calling you to become.

3. What new vision or alternative plan did the sermon offer for your journey?

4. State how the sermon helped you understand your present life's purpose.

5. As a result of the sermon, what is God calling you to do now?

Appendix G:
Developmental Behavior[185] in the Narrative Story

A. **What is the current behavior of the text?** The public actions?

B. **What is the probable behavior of the text?** What are people inclined to do/ leaning toward doing/being pulled and stretched to do/ probable actions?

---

[185] These questions were asked to seven young adults to help them assess reasons for behavior. This was a strategy to assist them in understanding the biblical narrative (In B. F. Skinner, *About Behaviorism* (New York, NY: Vintage Books, 1974), 29 – 32.

C. **What is the perceptual behavior of the text?** What do you see happening?

D. **What is the past behavior in the text?** Does yesterday actions connect with actions today?

E. **What is the covert behavior in the text?** What is not seen or hidden?

F. **What is the future behavior?** What are you going to do now?

Appendix H:
Frank Thomas' Method[186] of
Narrative Examination

Method used to determine the situation and celebration in the text

I. SITUATION: Examine the situation of the text. What is happening at the beginning of the story?

II. COMPLICATION: What is the Problem that the text points to? Sickness? Evil? Death? Sin?

---

[186] To help young adults understand the narrative of Ruth's 1 call to service, Dr. Frank Thomas' method of narrative examination was used to give young adults a procedure to understand the text and apply it to their present context. In Frank Thomas, *They Like To Never Quit Praisin' God* (Cleveland, OH: United Church Press, 1997).

III. RESOLUTION: How is the problem addressed and reversed by God?

IV. NEW VISION: What is the new way we are to think about the situation and complication?

V. GRACE APPEAL: What is the grace of the passage? What is the assurance and the affirmation of faith? What courage do we have?

VI. CELEBRATION: As a result of a redemptive past and a liberated future: What is the experience of victory? What is the empowerment? Who is set free? Encouraged? Healed? Saved?

V. TRANSFORMATION: What is the new thing we are to know and do?

Appendix I:
Robert Alter's Method of Narrative Interpretation

1) Identify the sense of suspense.[187]

2) Demonstrate the reversal and twist of our destiny.[188]

3) Name the demonic powers that need unmaking.[189]

4) List the continual revisions and multiple possibilities God presents in the story.[190]

5) Recognize the several theological and moral purposes and tendencies of God.[191]

6) Note the selectivity of specific words and significant variations of verbal formulas.[192]

---

[187] Robert Alter, *The Art of Biblical Narrative* (Berkeley, CA: Basic Books, 1981), 4.

[188] Ibid., 6.

[189] Ibid., 10.

[190] Ibid., 12.

[191] Ibid., 19.

[192] Ibid., 21.

7) Examine the contradictions and complexities in human life.[193]

8) Observe the dialectic reversals of thematic directions in the story.[194]

9) Study the narrative realizations that reveal the enactment of God's purposes in historical events.[195]

10) State the informing vision of God's design working through history[196] and your present context.

11) Inspect the patterns of repetition, symmetry, directional clues and what is innovative in the narrative.[197]

---

[193] Alter, 26.
[194] Ibid., 31.
[195] Ibid., 33.
[196] Ibid., 35.
[197] Ibid., 47.

Appendix J:
H. Michael Brewer's Hero Hermeneutic

Brewer's **hermeneutic of the hero** gives the **anatomy of heroic action.** Any ordinary person who longs for a rescuer or desires to be used by God can be a hero who delivers people from injustice and suffering[198] even on the smallest of levels.

1. Heroes are ordinary people who feel and experience failure.[199]

2. Heroes feel like losers, but God enables them to become winners.[200]

3. Heroes are called from shallowness and selfishness to accept their place as a hero.[201]

4. Heroes are called "to give something back to the world . . . to use [their] powers to aid others."[202]

---

[198] H. Michael Brewer, *Superheroes*, 10.
[199] Ibid., 39.
[200] Ibid., 105.
[201] Ibid., 106 – 107.
[202] Ibid., 108.

5. Heroes must become persons of self-sacrifice[203] who seek to take care of his/her neighbor.[204]

6. Heroes serve God by showing up and being available for God's use.[205]

7. God ***transforms*** the heroes weakness to power[206] to face the powers that hold people captive.

8. Heroes are called into God's service "to be good for something/ . . . to change the world/ . . . [to] improve the lives of people . . . and grow the world closer to God's vision of humanity."[207]

9. Heroes use their gifts trusting God to make them count.[208]

10. Heroes serve as role models to inspire and encourage others to use their gifts in the service of God.[209]

---

[203] Brewer, 41.
[204] Ibid., 66.
[205] Ibid., 114.
[206] Ibid., 92 – 93.
[207] Ibid., 110.
[208] Ibid., 115.
[209] Ibid., 117.

Appendix K:
Who is a Hero?[210]

Check the box that gives your understanding of a hero.

1. A hero is life-giving and gives healing power.

☐ **Yes** ☐ **No** ☐ **Uncertain**

2. A hero has been tested and passed the test.

☐ **Yes** ☐ **No** ☐ **Uncertain**

3. A hero is one who "faces and kills the dragon-terrors," the "tyrant-monsters."

☐ **Yes** ☐ **No** ☐ **Uncertain**

4. The hero submits to a difficult task for others.

☐ **Yes** ☐ **No** ☐ **Uncertain**

---

[210] Adapted from Joseph Campbell, *The Hero With A Thousand Faces* (Princeton, NJ: Princeton University Press, 1949).

5. The hero is limited but battles past limitations to inspire others.

☐ **Yes** ☐ **No** ☐ **Uncertain**

6. The hero goes into the world to transform it, renew it, and makes it a holy place.

☐ **Yes** ☐ **No** ☐ **Uncertain**

7. A hero is not a super star athlete or a pop star with money and a big name.

☐ **Yes** ☐ **No** ☐ **Uncertain**

8. A hero is a father, an uncle, a grandfather, a man who does not abandon or run out on his family.

☐ **Yes** ☐ **No** ☐ **Uncertain**

9. A hero is a man who will love, sacrifice, and gives what he has to better his family.

☐ **Yes** ☐ **No** ☐ **Uncertain**

10. A hero is a life-giver who offers himself sacrificially to build a better world for those who come after him.

☐ **Yes** ☐ **No** ☐ **Uncertain**

11. A Hero is one who brings light, understanding, and enlightenment to the mind and soul.

☐ **Yes** ☐ **No** ☐ **Uncertain**

12. A hero is one who will not turn back regardless of the difficulty of the task.

⬜ **Yes** ⬜ **No** ⬜ **Uncertain**

13. The hero overcomes his self-interests to revitalize the world.

⬜ **Yes** ⬜ **No** ⬜ **Uncertain**

Appendix L:
THE CALL TO BE A HERO!

Sermon Purpose:

Sermon Purpose: In view of many young adults who live on the margin of faith, I want to preach an apologetic sermon that invites young adults who are on the "outside" to become "insiders" to the church's mission of service and social transformation. It will be achieved by means of telling a narrative story that 1) addresses God's acceptance of us through grace, 2) God's call to use our giftedness and 3) our availability to used by God in ordinary ways, for service and social transformation, to help people to get on with the business of living.

Judges 6:7 – 16
Sunday, November 4, 2007

Charles Dickens, in his book, *A Tale of Two Cities*, penned the words,

> It was the best of times, it was the worst of times, / . . .it was the season of Light, it was

> the season of Darkness, it was the spring of
> hope, it was the winter of despair.[211]

It is usually in "the worst of times,/ . . . the season of darkness . . . [and] the winter of despair"[212] that we need heroes. When we *feel insignificant* we need a hero to tell us that we "were created for something greater, [we need a hero who we can] push to strive for big ideals and bigger dreams." [213] We need heroes to "walk beside us to see us through the perils of life/ . . . So we keep looking for heroes."[214]

In chapter 6:7 of Judges, the people of Israel have seen the best of times and the worst of times. They have been constantly impoverished by the Medianites, a group of "thugs" who were Amorite gangsters who constantly rob them, demean them, and terrorize them. In the face of these dehumanizing conditions, the people of Israel *cried out* to the Lord for a deliver.

In verse 8, the Bible declares that *God sent them a prophet*. The prophet reminded them of God's history of deliverance and rescue. In the words of the Spirituals, the

---

[211] Charles Dickens, "A Tale of Two Cities," accessed 2 November 2007, <http://www.quotationspage.com/quotes/Charles_Dickens.html>.

[212] Ibid.

[213] Leo Partible in H. Michael Brewer, *Who Needs a Superhero? Finding Virtue, Vice, and What's Holy in the Comics* (Grand Rapids, MI: Baker Books, 2004), 5, 7.

[214] H. Michael Brewer, *Who Needs a Superhero? Finding Virtue, Vice, and What's Holy in the Comics* (Grand Rapids, MI: Baker Books, 2004), 9.

prophet declared, "If God delivered Daniel, surely God can deliver me." In Gideon's story, we hear God calling us to ***heroic action***. In verse 11, Gideon, the son of Joash, is ***an unlikely candidate to be a hero.*** He is unknown; he is from a poor family; he describes himself as the least, the last and the youngest in his family. Yet, in our longing for a hero, ***Gideon will do***. Look at Gideon:

- o   He has ***no mission statement*** like ***Superman*** – "to save the world."[215]

- o   He has ***no inner power*** like ***Bruce Banner*** who becomes the ***"Hulk."***[216]

- o   He has ***no catch phrase*** like ***Billy Batson*** who in the utterance of the words ***"Shazam"*** is transformed into ***Captain Marvel*** who has ***Solomon's*** wisdom, ***Hercules's*** strength, ***Atlas's*** stamina, ***Zeus's power***, ***Achilles's*** courage, and ***Mercury's*** speed.[217]

- o   Unlike ***Bruce Wayne***, The Batman, Gideon has no "cape," no "uniform," no "camouflage," no "tactical planning," and no "talent   . . . [that] demands our admiration and respect."[218] Yet, Gideon will have to do.

Gideon, like us, is an unlikely hero. In verse 11, he goes about his daily work threshing wheat and hiding from the Midianites. He works and he hides out of fear of ***what***

---

[215] Brewer, 14.
[216] Ibid., 24.
[217] Ibid., 93.
[218] Ibid., 36 – 37.

they will take from him. He hides fearing ***what they will do*** to him. When he hides, he is limited, stifled, hindered, pushed down, constrained and confined from his true potential.

Yet, in verse 12, the word of God found him and declared – "The Lord is with you, you mighty man of valour." When we are hiding, God finds us and calls us mighty. The Lord is with you ***"mighty one," "strong warrior," "mighty man and woman of fearless courage."***

In verse 12, ***God finds Gideon where he is*** – He is "hiding," and "fearful." Yet, God declares ***who he is to be*** – "a person of valor, boldness, and courage." Where ever you are hiding, God finds you to declare to you that you are a person of significance, purpose, and unique gifts that can save the day.[219]

When the word of God found Gideon, it came ***to transform*** him into a hero. God's word comes to us to change us, strengthen us, and engage us in small and meaningful causes. In the comic book hero series, ***Don Blake*** was a frail man. Yet, when people cried out for help, ***Don Blake*** would ***kneel down*** and strike his walking stick upon the ground and in a blinding flash his unimpressive figure would disappear and he would be the steel-muscled mighty Thor.[220]

In times of need, God calls you to ***kneel down*** and ***allow God to transform your frailty*** into ***mighty***. God called

---

[219] Brewer, 14.
[220] Ibid., 92.

Gideon to be mighty and God is calling us to be mighty. To be mighty is *to be "serviceable;* to be mighty is to *do something"*[221] that will *make a difference;* to be mighty is to *be "responsible"* and "good for something."[222]

God calls you "mighty." You are a person of *"valor"* and you are a person of *"value"* to God. God's message to *Gideon and to Gidget* is – *"You are accepted!"* In spite of your age, your background, your faults, your failings, your insecurity, or how you feel about yourself, *God accepts you.*

- o   God accepts you when you don't accept yourself.[223]

- o   God accepts you when you are full of "guilt" and have no meaning in your life."[224]

- o   God accepts you to bring you to who you fully can become.[225]

Why does God accept me? God accepts because God is *graceful* and *grace - filled. Grace* is the compassionate love of God that seeks me out and finds me; grace gives me what I could not earn; and grace gives me what I could never deserve.

---

[221] John Goldingay, *Models for Interpretation of Scripture* (Grand Rapids, MI: William B. Eerdmans Publishing Company, 1995), 7.

[222] Brewer, 110.

[223] Paul Tillich, "You are Accepted," *The Shaking of the Foundations* (New York, NY: Charles Scribner's Sons, 1948), 153, 154, 155.

[224] Ibid., 158.

[225] Ibid.

o God accepts me to deliver me from my worst self.

o God accepts me to change my destiny[226] and direction.

o God accepts me to break the powers that hold me in the despair and hopelessness.[227]

o God accepts me to free me from feelings of emptiness and doubt.[228]

In this story, **God accepts Gideon but Gideon was slow to accept God.** In verse 13, **Gideon complained** that God was not getting anything done in his community. Gideon asked God, "Why is all of this stuff happening to us? Where are your miracles? Why have you abandoned us?"

God's answer to Gideon's **was Gideon**. In verse 14, **God called Gideon to be a hero.** Verse 14 reads, "And the Lord looked upon him, and said, Go in this thy might, and thou shalt save Israel." The good news is, the Lord looks upon you, both young and old to save your Israel.

God declared– "Gideon you are answer to the problems, issues, and concerns around you. You have the power to pull people out of their stuck condition and get them going again." God called Gideon and God "Expect[ed] to get something done in life"[229] through Gideon's work.

---

[226] Tillich, *The Shaking*,158.

[227] Ibid., 160.

[228] Ibid.

[229] Harry Emerson Fosdick, "What Is the Matter with Preaching," In Mike Graves (ed.), *What's the Matter with Preaching Today?* (Louisville, KY: Westminster John Knox Press, 2004), 17.

God's answer to the "mess" of your context is "you." God says to you and to me, "Go and save your Israel, your home, your school, your family, the boy or girl on the street where you live." ***You are the good news*** God that has prepared for the world.

The ***call of the hero*** is a call that declares, "You are needed by God to use your gifts, in small acts of faithfulness to do what needs to be done to transform life.[230] In verse 16, God tells Gideon, "Surely, I will be with you." You can be a hero because ***the God who calls you is with you.***

Whether you are on the "inside," or on the "outside" of the church, ***God is calling you*** and God will be with you.

- o Yes, ordinary, quiet and overlooked person, God will be with you.
- o God wants to use your gifts to do what needs to be done.[231]
- o In spite of your feelings of failure, God will be with you.[232]
- o When you feel like a loser, God will be with you.[233]
- o God will enable you "to give something back to the world . . . to aid others."[234] God will be with you.

---

[230] Brewer, 112, 114.
[231] Ibid., 118.
[232] Ibid., 39.
[233] Ibid., 105.
[234] Ibid., 108.

Since God is "with you," ***you are called to be "with God."*** How can I be with God?

o   Be with God by ***being available***.[235]

o   Be with God by ***showing up*** "to change the world/ [and]. . . [to] improve the lives of people."[236]

o   Be with God by ***serving as a role model*** to inspire and encourage others to use their gifts in the service of God.[237]

In a news article in the <u>Chicago Defender</u>, the article read that the Chicago Bears defensive tackle Tommie Harris:

> . . . realizes true life is really bigger than the 100 yards he works on each Sunday."[238] Harris wants to devote himself to helping "young people who are dying due to senseless violence." Harris stated that he wants to go after crime and he wants to do something through his charitable foundation.[239]

> Harris wants to help young people have a different mind set. He wants to "construct youth centers, start Big Brother programs, provide an alternative to the streets and

---

[235] Brewer, 114.

[236] Ibid., 110.

[237] Ibid., 117.

[238] Larry Gross, "Bears Star Wants to Help Sack Crime in City," *Chicago Defender*, 29 – 30 October 2007, 24.

[239] Ibid.

show kids how to build a better life."[240] Harris stated, "As athletes, we have been blessed. We have an obligation to share those blessings."[241]

God is calling you to be a hero. God is calling you to ***be a blessing*** to gives someone the advantage, a hand up, and a push up; God wants you to be a blessing to ***encourage*** someone,[242] to ***connect*** with someone who is disconnected, and to ***point*** someone to the Lord Jesus as the answer to the problems that distract their lives.[243]

- o Be a hero by listening to people.
- o Be a hero by serving people.
- o Be a hero by praying for someone.
- o Be a hero by lifting someone up to be their best.
- o Be a hero by bringing laughter into someone's life.
- o Be a hero by caring[244] for someone.

---

[240] Gross, 24.

[241] Ibid.

[242] Brewer, 97.

[243] Fosdick, 8.

[244] Responses to a pre - questionnaire on "The Call of a Hero." 1) Who is your favorite Hero? 2) What is your hero's greatest gift and ability? 3) What is your greatest gift and ability? (Sunday, October 28, 2007).

Pre – Questionnaire on the Sermon
"The Call of a Hero"

This questionnaire has three questions. The answers submitted are in a, b, c, order. Each letter represents the respondent to the hero stated.

What was revealing was the number of young people who saw people in the church and their parents as heroes. This was encouraging to me. Second, many of the young people were able to identify their ability and gift to help others.

Who is your favorite hero?	What is your hero's greatest gift/ability?	What is your greatest ability?
Superman	b. Helping people no matter the cost. g. Has strength, can fly, and is smart. l. Strong, handsome, and save people. m. She helps people.	b. Being able to talk to people and helping them. g. I am smart, funny, and can make people laugh. l. I am smart and work hard to succeed. m. Smart in math and sometimes funny.
Hulk		
Batman	f. Focused on how to catch criminals.	f. I can motivate people.

Iron Man		
Wonder Woman	k. Strong, brave, courageous, and saves people in danger.	k. I am smart, loving, and strive to do my best.
Bionic Woman		
Spider Man	p. Can shoot webs out of his wrists.	p. I have good handwriting.
X – Men		
Dr. Martin King, Jr.	a. Ability to be peaceful in adversity.	a. Caring, giving, sharing
Jesus	c. Dying for my sins. d. He saves. p. Leads people in the path of righteousness and protects me.	c. To serve God and serve Christ. d. Hope, pray, faith p. I believe in my hero.
M. Bowden	e. She can sing and can make you feel good.	e. Helping others and babysitting.
My mom	h. Making meals	h. Eating
Mom	i. Nice, helpful	i. I help, share, and care.
Harry Potter	j. Gift of love, leadership, knowledge	j. Gift of understanding and singing, writing.

Mom & Dad	n. Loving, caring, responsible	n. loving, caring
Mom and Grandmother	o. Their strength, they are never weak in any kind of way.	o. I can play any sport.
M. Johnson	q. Singing and helping	q. Helping others any way I can.

Appendix M:
Sermon Outlines on Service and Social Transformation

The two following sermon outlines were preached to assist young people in hearing God's call upon their lives with a challenge to take their heroic place in service and social transformation. These outlines are offered as an illustration of how the biblical narrative can inform young people of God's appointment and placement of their lives in heroic service to others and social transformation.

Sermon:
"God is Calling You to Commitment"
Ruth 1:1 – 8, 10 – 11, 14, 16 – 18

There is a ***crisis arises*** in the family. Elimelech dies and Naomi is left with two sons. As the young men grow up, they marry two young women in the town, Ruth and Orpah. For the next ten years, it appears like a story book conclusion, and then both of the sons die.

I. Naomi, Ruth, and Orpah face a crisis of death and insecurity.

A. No pension, no insurance, no annuity, no social security.

B. In the face of their **problems,** these women held things together.

C. **What complications are you facing?**

   1. Are you unemployed?

   2. Are you battling with a crisis of sickness?

   3. Are you in a "stuck" situation without hope or direction?

II. Naomi refused to stay stuck.

A. Naomi teaches us, **"Don't Park in Your Crisis.**

B. Whatever your calamity, you might start there, but don't stay there.

C. Naomi did not park in her pain. She "looked ahead" and "moved forward."

III. **Naomi had a new vision** beyond her present condition.

A. She received news that **there was bread in Bethlehem.**

   1. That vision inspired her, and focused her on God's purpose.[245]

---

[245] George Barna, *The Power of Team Leadership* (Colorado Springs, CO: Waterbrook Press, 2001), 37 – 39.

B. Naomi moved forward, but did not force Ruth & Orpah to do the same.

   1. Naomi offers Ruth and Orpah an opportunity to go home to Moab.

   2. Orpah chooses to go home, but Ruth *"identified" with Naomi.*

   Ruth said, "Don't force me to leave you; don't make me go home. Where you go, I go; and where you live, I'll live. Your people are my people, your God is my god; where you die, I'll die, and that's where I'll be buried, so help me GOD—not even death itself is going to come between us!"

C. *Ruth was connected with Naomi* – "Don't force me to leave you."

   1. Ruth makes a choice to commit herself to Naomi.

   2. She will not abandon her.

D. What was Ruth committed to?

   1. She was committed to a *new direction* – "Where you go I will go."

   2. Ruth was *committed to a new way of living* – "Where you live, I will live."

   3. Ruth was *committed to a new community* – "Your people will be my people."

   4. Ruth was *committed to a new God relationship* – "Your God will be my God."

5. Ruth had experienced a transformed life with Naomi. Naomi helped Ruth experience a "redeemed past and a liberated future" [246] in God.

IV. *Finally,* Ruth was *committed to a new destiny* – "Where you die, I will die."

    A. Ruth affirms her new destiny will not be where she started.

    B. Ruth will not die in an old way of life; she will go forward in faith free from her past fears and anxieties.[247]

    C. Ruth's destiny is to trust in the Lord.

    D. The question is *what will you commit to?*

        1. Will you commit to the uncertainties and the negations of life?[248]

        2. Will you commit to fear and frustration?

        3. Or will you, with courage, like Ruth take a step of faith and commit your life to the Lord Jesus Christ who can change your destiny and use you, like Ruth in salvation purposes?

---

[246] Frank Thomas, *They Like to Never Quit Praisin' God* (Cleveland, OH: United Church Press, 1997), 46.

[247] Ibid., 59.

[248] Ibid., 27.

Sermon:
"Take Your Place with the Bruised"
Luke 4:16 – 18

V 18c "The Spirit of the Lord is upon me to/ . . . set at liberty them that are bruised."

In Tyler Perry's movie, ***Ma Dear's Family Reunion***, a family of children born of slaves gather for a family reunion. At the end of the movie, the bell is rung from the cabin of the family ancestors. As the generations gather at the porch, Cicily Tyson who portrays one of the elder women, shout outs – "Young men, take your place! Young women, take your place! Take your place! Take your place!"

I. Jesus returns to His home in Nazareth.

    A. He enters a worship service.

    B. In the worship Jesus "takes His place" in a ***mission of social transformation*** "to . . . set at liberty them that are bruised."

II. ***Life is full of bruises***. Throughout our childhood our activities and play there are scrapes, scratches, cuts, slashes, and gashes. After every bruise, we run to our mothers who kiss the bruise, clean it, and start us on our way again.

    A. ***Financial bruises*** to which we look for bankers to heal.

    B. ***Educational bruises*** that we hope teachers can heal.

C. ***Emotional and psychological*** bruises that we pray counselors can heal.

D. ***Family and relational bruises*** that we go to Judge Judy to heal.

III. The good news, in the text, is Jesus brings a reversal and a twist in our dilemma.[249]

A. He unmasks and suspends[250] the powers that have bruised us.

B. He brings a dramatic shift in our distress and our destination.

C. He sets us free from our bruises.

D. ***What does it mean to be bruised?***

1. ***bruised (molops)*** means ***to swell*** from being beaten unjustly.[251]

2. ***bruised (thrauo)*** means ***to be broken into pieces***.[252]

3. ***bruised (suntribo)*** means to be thrown against something (a wall).[253]

---

[249] Robert Alter, *The Art of Biblical Narrative* (Berkeley, CA: Basic Books, 1981), 6.

[250] Ibid., 10, 12.

[251] Geoffrey Bromiley, *Theological Dictionary of the New Testament* (Grand Rapids, MI: William B. Eerdmans Publishing Company, 1985), 619.

[252] Spiro Zodhiates, *The Complete Word Study Dictionary: New Testament* (Chattanooga, TN: AMG Publishers, 1992), 741.

[253] Ibid., 1346.

E. Whatever your situation, Jesus has come to set you free from your bruise.

IV. ***What does it mean to be "set at liberty?"***

A. To be ***set (lyo) at liberty*** is to be untied and unwrapped from the binding and chaining of Satan. [254]

B. To be ***set at liberty (eleutheroo)*** is to be free from what enslaves you.[255]

C. To be ***set (kineo) at liberty*** is to be put into motion.[256]

D. To be ***set (anago) at liberty*** means to alter one's course and to be navigated and to set sail[257] in a new direction.

Alvin Richardson[258] declares we have been set free from our bruises to ***take our place*** in the "vision of ***God's design***"[259] for our lives. He pens the words,

> I can hear a sound,/ something reaching out to me,/ Calling me to be everything that I'm designed to be./ I will not deny the voice I hear inside/ telling me of my destiny and the purpose for my life./

---

[254] Bromiley, 148.

[255] Ibid., 224.

[256] Ibid., 435.

[257] Ibid., 146

[258] Alvin Richardson, Jr., "Destiny," *Leader's Songbook: The Jesus Way* (Chicago, IL: Urban Ministries, Inc., 2007), 2.

[259] Alter, 35.

Somehow I know that the moment has arrived,/ and I know that I'm ready and now is the time.

This is my time,/ this is my destiny,/ to choose the path that has been chosen for me./ My hopes and dreams are waiting there for me./ This is my destiny.

V. *What is your destiny?*

A. Your destiny is to join the Lord Jesus in *the liberating business*.

B. Your mission is to set someone at liberty from their bruises.

C. Go forward and loose someone and *provide comfort* for their affliction and suffering.[260]

D. Now is the time to *take our place* with the bruised.

    1. Take our place in Christ to *reverse the discrepancies* of life in our homes and at school.

    2. Take our place in *correcting the conflicts* that have afflicted people at work and the playground.

The following two sermon outlines were preached to awaken the heroic consciousness in young adults to their true pursuit of service. Following the outlines, I will offer

---

[260] Bromiley, 170.

insights I gleaned from these biblical hero narratives and why they were important for anyone using this method.

Sermon: Luke 15:11 - 19
"The Pursuit of Happiness"

Sermon Purpose:

This sermon will attempt to encourage young adults to take responsibility for their "far country" journeys by being awakened early to the call of God to serviceable as they journey toward accepting adult growth and responsibility. Happiness is found in one's relational connection to the Lord Jesus Christ.

In this story, a young son wanted a "piece of the pie." What motivated this young son to make the request? Did he want to better his condition? Be upwardly mobile? Do something different? Or just get out on his own?[261]

I. In his rush for the pursuit of happiness, the young son *"packed his bags and left for* the *far country."*

A. Why did this young pursue the far county?

B. Was he "looking for a good time,"[262] "a better life,"[263] or a place he could do whatever he

---

[261] Reflections on the Preaching Peer Group in their thoughts on why the young hero in Luke 15:11 – 12 wanted his inheritance from his father, January 3, 2007.

[262] Delores, an adult respondent, responds to why the young hero in the text went into the far country, Luke 15:12 – 14, January 19, 2007.

[263] Theodore, a 16 year old, responds to why the young hero in the text went into the far country, Luke 15:12 – 14, January 19, 2007.

wanted without his father looking over his shoulder?[264]

C. Did this young hero start out with a "life plan?"[265]

D. Did he begin his journey in a search for "something worth living for?"[266]

II. In his pursuit of pleasure, "he had spent all in riotous living."

A. ***Riotous living (asotia)*** is "extravagant squandering of one's resources by spending too much."

B. ***Riotous living*** is "spending freely on one's own lusts and appetites."

C. ***Riotous living*** is a lack of self-restraint in lust, pleasure, drunkenness, and debauchery.[267]

D. In his pursuit of pleasure, ***where he hoped to go, he did not end up***.

---

[264] Cherrelle, a 17 year old, responds to why the young hero in the text went into the far country, Luke 15:12 – 14, January 19, 2007.

[265] Erik H. Erikson, *Childhood and Society* (New York, NY: W. W. Norton and Company, 1963), 150.

[266] Dean, *Practicing Passion*, 9.

[267] Spiros Zodhiates, *The Complete Word Study Dictionary: New Testament* (Chattanooga, TN: AMG Publishers, 1992), 284

1. He found himself living in a deficit, "discontented, alienated, and empty."[268]

2. In the field with the pigs, he was engaged in ***ragged and wretched living***.

III. Coming to himself, the young son pursued a real relationship.

A. "I will arise and go to my father."

B. This ***young man's pursuit of happiness*** was found in his father.

C. On his way home, he states his new pursuit of happiness, "make me as one of thy hired servants."

D. To be happy, he was willing to be serviceable and accountable.[269]

E. He was on his way to becoming ***a servant – hero***

1. He would ***(diakoneo)*** "wait at a table."

2. He would ***(diakonein)*** "supervise, provide, and prepare a meal in love.[270]

3. He would ***(therapeuo)*** be serviceable to

[268] Carol Pearson, *Awakening the Heroes Within* (New York, NY: Harper Collins Publishers, 1991), 123.

[269] Roger Connors, Tome Smith, and Craig, Hickman, *The Oz Principle* (New York, NY: The Penguin Group, 2004), 14.

[270] Bromiley, *Theological Dictionary*, 153.

the sick.[271]

4. He would *(hierougeo)* "perform sacred or sacrificial ministry"[272] in temple,[273] in prayer,[274] and teaching religious instruction.[275]

5. He would *(leitourgeo)* do a task for society at his own expense.

F. To desire to be a servant is to be awakened to the heroic. This young son became a hero when he discovered the meaning of his life at his father's house was service.

Sermon
1 SAMUEL 17:30 – 40
"YOU CAN BE A HERO TOO!"

Sermon Purpose

In view of the many young people who are stuck in a crisis of mission and purpose, I want to help the young adults become aware of their God called mission to "do something" to help people unstuck from their crisis situations. The challenge is accept one's personal mission and take actions to be of service to others. I will achieve this by telling a story narrative that leads to 1) an awareness

[271] Bromiley, 331.
[272] Ibid., 354.
[273] Ibid., 354.
[274] Ibid., 355.
[275] Ibid., 356.

of one's personal mission, 2) use one's skills and abilities to face large and small challenges that are ahead, and 3) to take actions to enable others to get unstuck from their crisis situations.

There was a popular cola commercial that said, "I'm a Pepper; He's a Pepper, and you can be a Pepper too!" In this story of David, we can insert the words, "I'm a hero; she's a hero, and you can be a hero too!"

I. David's encounter with Goliath is our ongoing struggle against the demonic powers.

    A. Forty days, Goliath challenged the army of Israel to combat.

    B. Young David was moved to "do something."

II. ***David wanted to be a hero.***

    A. David told Saul, "Don't give up hope, I'm ready to go and fight this Philistine."

    B. David's readiness to fight calls us to ***come to the front line*** and ***make an impact.***[276]

    C. David was ready to get ***unstuck*** and moving again.

---

[276] Andy Stanley et. al. *Seven Practices of Practical Ministry.* Sisters, OR: Multnomah Publishers, 2004), 159. Upon reflection of the sermon (January 18, 2006), the Preaching Peer Group suggested a definition of "impact." An impact is to have a collision that causes something to alter its course. An impact pushes something in another direction. An impact expands something beyond its present horizons and capacities to do more. An impact is a continuous enlightening.

D. David was willing to "do something" to benefit others.

E. The call is for Davids and Dividas to come to the front line

  1. To experience servant leadership.

  2. To get involved.

  3. To ***be part of a revolution*** that changes lives.[277]

III. David teaches us ***it takes courage to challenge Goliath***.

The following is a story of courage for in an article titled "Everyday Heroes."[278]

> Jeff May was a student at Columbine High School when a young man in a black trench coat began shooting and killing students. Jeff, armed with only a pencil, ran at the gunman to stop him. One of the teachers declared that Jeff's actions saved his classmates lives.

You can be a hero by using what is in your hand to get people unstuck from their crisis situations. You can ***encourage someone*** to never "give up," or "give in." Giants keep coming, but ***David's and Davidas*** keep coming also.

---

[277] Stanley et al, 159.

[278] Tom Spitz and Layne Kennedy, "Everyday Heroes: The Student," *Reader's Digest*, January 2006, 30.

Appendix N:
You Can Be a Hero Too!

What I have discovered in my attempts to preach narratives of the heroic to young adults is, not only are they awakened, but the heroic consciousness of older adults are awakened also. Dr. Jack Skiles, my advisor to this project, in a sermon titled, "Courage to Stand Tall" summarized, in this sermon, his observations of this preaching initiative of "Telling the Story to Awaken the Hero Within." His reflection and declaration of "my story" and journey is a heroic act to which I am grateful:

> Can you imagine with me what the surprise has been out of his project in preaching? It has been twofold really. First, he discovered he needed to be more one-on-one with his young people. Preaching from the perch of the pulpit, no matter how powerfully, does not ever preclude needing to stop and listen most sincerely to the lives, the worries, the dreams of the young people we want to cause to stand up in our midst to be our future leaders. He has discovered the joy of

connection with his young people that will probably be the key that serves to unlock his church into openly welcoming the new ventures that these young people will carry into the next generations of ministry.

But the surprise that struck this preacher of many years was that when he preached to bring to new life to the [young] Davids who will take on the giants, the Goliaths of today's world, when he examined the tenacity in II Kings 22 of the prophetess Huldah who challenged young King Josiah to bring reform to the Jewish nation—do you know who stood up and said, "Here I am, Use Me?" You do. It was the old folks. It was retired folks. The tired folks. The folks who felt that they had been used up and dried up and put away for burial.

The preacher named Radio has discovered in his church that all those old brittle bones rattling around every Sunday as in Ezekiel's valley of dried bones—that by faithfully preaching the stories of biblical heroes who found their strength coming from God, God's movement in their lives has produced new hope, new vigor and new direction, in addition to the young people's dreaming dreams of what God will yet accomplish through their faithfully lived lives.[279]

---

[279] Jack Skiles, 26 August 2007. "Courage to Stand Tall," (Jeremiah 1:4 – 10; Luke 13:10 – 17), <http://www. firstunitedchurchbloomington.org/sundayworship/sermon_new. html> Accessed 1 September 2007.